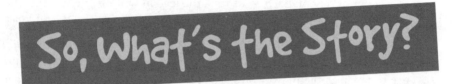

So, What's the Story?

A note on the Exceeding the Common Core State Standards series:

We undertook this series of three books (*Get It Done! Writing and Analyzing Informational Texts to Make Things Happen*; *Oh, Yeah?! Putting Argument to Work Both in School and Out*; *So, What's the Story? Teaching Narrative to Understand Ourselves, Others, and the World*) as a collaborative project designed to share our ideas on how to teach the three types of writing addressed by the Common Core State Standards in such a way that students will develop the knowledge they need to do important work both in and out of school. Each of us took the lead in writing one volume; the other two made or suggested a variety of revisions. We are able to work together because we share so much about what we think makes good writing and good teaching, so you'll see many, many similarities across the books, especially in the central principles we use to organize them. But you'll also see some differences in our approaches and in our points of emphasis. To paraphrase Mark Twain, we make this explanation for the reason that without it many readers would suppose that all three authors were trying to talk alike and not succeeding.

So, What's the Story?

Teaching Narrative to Understand Ourselves, Others, and the World

James E. Fredricksen

Jeffrey D. Wilhelm

Michael W. Smith

HEINEMANN
Portsmouth, NH

Heinemann
361 Hanover Street
Portsmouth, NH 03801–3912
www.heinemann.com

Offices and agents throughout the world

The authors and publisher wish to thank those who have generously given permission to reprint borrowed material:

Excerpts from *Common Core State Standards* © Copyright 2010. National Governors Association Center for Best Practices and Council of Chief State School Officers. All rights reserved.

Library of Congress Cataloging-in-Publication Data
Fredricksen, James E.
    So, what's the story? : teaching narrative to understand ourselves, others, and the world / James E. Fredricksen, Jeffrey D. Wilhelm, and Michael W. Smith.
        p.   cm.
    Includes bibliographical references and index.
    ISBN-13: 978-0-325-04292-3
    ISBN-10: 0-325-04292-6
    1. English language—Composition and exercises—Study and teaching. 2. Narration (Rhetoric)—Study and teaching.   I. Wilhelm, Jeffrey D.   II. Smith, Michael W.   III. Title.

LB1576.F726 2012
372.6—dc23   2012021745

Editor: Samantha Bennett
Production: Vicki Kasabian
Interior and cover designs: Monica Crigler
Typesetter: Kim Arney
Manufacturing: Steve Bernier

Printed in the United States of America on acid-free paper
16 15 14 13 12 ML 1 2 3 4 5

To Bill and Cheryl Fredricksen
Those notes left in lunch bags and those letters
written on graph paper left waiting for me
on the kitchen counter most mornings after
you worked the late-night shifts . . .
well, they're why I teach writing and writers.
Literacy is love: You taught me that.
And much more.

Contents

Acknowledgments

Jim would like to thank cowriters Jeff Wilhelm and Michael Smith, who do this kind of work the right way—through collaboration and by thinking, writing, and reading hard and with compassion. Thanks to Samantha Bennett, our editor, for her encouraging words, and thanks to the team at Heinemann who made this book come to life. Much gratitude goes to the many teachers who shared their stories with us—some made it into the book and some did not—you all live the idea that our profession only strengthens when we share our work with one another: Rachel Bear, Bruce Ballenger, Emily Morgan, Mitch Nobis, Rick Cook, Greg Wilson, Sarah Woodard, Jessie Craft, Christine Voreis, Beth Harris, Deb Marsh, Lauren Nizol, Christine O'Neil, and the entire Middleton Thinking Partner Team (Kim Brocke, Jayna Eichelberger, Cheryl Forse, Robin Renee Gilbert, Jelena Maxwell, Nicole Mitchell, Gretchen Smith, and Angela Young). Also, many thanks to the National Writing Project for creating opportunities for educators to share, honor, and develop their expertise, including all the people involved with the Literacy in the Common Core initiative. The LCC Leadership Team includes Tanya Baker, Rebeca Garcia-Gonzalez, Elyse Eidman-Aadahl, Michael Thompson, Cindy O'Donnell-Allen, Marcie Wolfe, Linda Denstaedt, Laura Schiller, Jean Wolph, Melanie Hammer, Brandy D'Alba, and Rachel Bear. Thanks to all teachers on the state teams, including the team members from Idaho—Anna Daley, Rachel Bear, Cecilia Pattee, Sarah Veigel, Andrew Porter, and James LeDoux. Thanks to Jim's students and colleagues from Fairfield, St. Charles, Michigan State, Boise State, and the Boise State Writing Project—there are far too many to name, but know that he listened to and learned from you. And to people who read long, rambling emails and in-process drafts, including Jim's writing group: Leah Zuidema, Anne Whitney, and Troy Hicks, and also Paula Uriarte, Jess Westhoff, and especially Rachel Bear.

Finally, much love and many thanks to Jim's brother and his family (Bill, Julie, Marley, and Makenzie Fredricksen) and to Jim's sister and her family (Nicole, Jake, Wyatt, and Porter Snopko). You make Jim's story and, in turn, his life a better one. He couldn't be any luckier or more grateful.

Jeff thanks Connie Bates for her continuous kindness and support over the course of many years and always at the right time. Gratitude goes to the fellows of the Boise State Writing Project and the members of the CCSS national implementation team. Particular thanks go to Rachel Bear, Anna Daley, Angie Young, Erika Boas, Cecilia Soto-Pattee, Frank Dehoney, and Brandon Bolyard. Thanks too to the National Writing Project for all its leadership and support, particularly Tanya Baker. Thanks, as always, to friends like Brian White and Deb Appleman, who are supportive in so many professional and personal ways. And continuous gratitude to his wife Peggy Jo Wilhelm and daughters Fiona Luray and Jasmine Marie, for inspiration, love, and daily displays of courage, fortitude and true human heroism

Michael thanks the Chicago crew with whom he's shared so many stories and so many ideas about how to teach students to write them, especially George Hillocks Jr., Steve Gevinson, the late Larry Johannessen, Betsy Kahn, Carol Lee, Steve Littell, Tom Mc-Cann, Peter Smagorinsky, and Carolyn Calhoun Walter. Thanks, too, to Brian White for an ongoing dialogue (over twenty years now!) about the stories that matter most and to his colleagues at the College of Education at Temple University for making the college such a congenial environment in which to work. Finally, as always, thanks to his wonderfully supportive wife, Karen Flynn, his daughters Catherine and Rachel, and his granddaughter Gabrielle who give meaning to all that he does.

An Introduction to Our Approach

We make sense of our world by piecing together stories.
—Nick Morgan

ll three of us are storytellers, both informally and formally. Informally, we often tell stories of what is happening in our personal and professional lives. Just today, Jeff told a colleague the story of a seventh-grade class that specializes in comic complaints and excuses. Jim swapped stories with colleagues at other National Writing Project sites about lessons that flopped miserably. Michael regaled his wife Karen with a story about how he coped with an office so cold, he claimed, that you could almost see your breath.

More formally, Michael and Jeff have been telling teacher research stories about student engagement, particularly focusing on how to engage boys and about how to engage and teach struggling readers and writers to sophisticated performances. Jim spins narratives about how teachers talk to each other in different situations and what is accomplished by the different kinds of talk he has documented.

You see, we're all storytellers, even if we haven't published a story in a professional journal or on NPR or on television. We've told stories since we were young, and we learned about life through the tales we heard and the stories we shared. *Once upon a time* and . . . *and then . . . and then . . . and then . . .* and *the end* are common phrases for signaling a story that are understood by the very young to the very elderly.

The Challenge and Promise of Teaching Narrative

Here's a complication though: telling a story is one thing, and writing a story is another. It takes a high level of awareness to understand how stories are shaped and how they shape the way people see the world, understand themselves and others, and consider choices about the future. As our title suggests, *So, What's the Story? Teaching Narrative to Understand Ourselves, Others, and the World* focuses not just on storytelling but also on what it means for someone to intentionally compose a narrative and on how composing (and reading) stories can help young people understand the way narrative concepts might help them identify, critique, and ultimately change their world.

This might seem like a lofty claim, but we think narrative permeates and both explicitly and implicitly informs so much of our lives and so much of the way cultures operate that teaching narrative has to be about much more than the form of a story—that is, it has to be about more than identifying the protagonist or naming the climax of a story or using the Freytag Pyramid (or Freytag Triangle, if you prefer) to figure out what was or what needs to be included in a story. Indeed, we think that narrative concepts can help people inquire into their world and that the best way to understand narrative concepts is to compose narratives. Put another way, we believe that composing is one way to discover (not just demonstrate) what one knows about a set of concepts (like narrative concepts) and that the purpose for discovering and developing one's understanding of those concepts is to help people participate in their communities in ways that make the community and the storyteller healthier.

Readers of our previous books, and particularly of the other two books in this series on teaching narrative, argument, and informational texts in ways that will meet and exceed the new Common Core State Standards (CCSS), will know that the *telos*, or overarching goal, for our teaching is that it not only leads to achieving the standards but also actually helps students to engage and do functional and democratic work in their classroom, school, community, and world.

Marshall Ganz, a lecturer at Harvard's Kennedy School of Government, writes that stories matter because they help us see what we think is important. "The way we talk about this [hope] is not just to go up to someone and say, 'Be hopeful,'" he writes. "We don't just talk about hope and other values in abstractions. We talk about them in the language of stories because stories are what enable us to communicate these values to one another" (Ganz 2009).

We suspect you agree with us that stories matter in both small and incredibly large ways, but we also suspect that you might feel overwhelmed too. "How do I teach story writing?" "I know it's important, but I just don't have time." "I know (scientists, historians, artists, athletes, mathematicians, etc.) tell stories to understand and solve problems and are understood through stories, but I have content to teach." "I don't have time to teach writing, let alone story writing to my students." "But the tests don't emphasize stories" (or a variation, "But the test values overly formulaic stories"). We've heard these questions and feelings of uncertainty and of anxiety for years, including from ourselves.

The Challenge and Promise of the CCSS

On top of these concerns we now face a new challenge with the CCSS. All three of us are heavily involved in reviewing the CCSS and helping teachers to implement them. And though we share some of the critiques that have been offered, our quibbles are minor. We want to go on record as saying that we like the CCSS very much, and we think they offer the greatest opportunity we have seen in our careers for professionalizing teachers and for helping our students be more engaged and competent readers, writers, and problem solvers. Consistent with the last forty-plus years of research in cognitive science, the CCSS focuses on the procedures of learning. This leaves the content to teachers. That means we get to choose what materials and curricular frameworks will best leverage developing the identified procedures for our particular students in our particular classrooms and communities. That makes the CCSS a momentous opportunity for professional decision making.

Here's another of the many things we like about the CCSS: The standards are few and are vertically aligned. That means that teachers from grades K–12 will be working together to help students master the same few generative processes of expert readers, writers, and learners in the disciplines. This vertical alignment means that students are much more likely to have a coherent curriculum and experience during their time in school, even if they move to another community or state that is using the CCSS, as forty-five states and the District of Columbia have agreed to do as of this writing. And here's something else: Because there are standards for literacy in the disciplines, all teachers in all content areas are going to be part of the same enterprise of creating literate students, students who will know how to read, write, and think like a democratic citizen, scientist, historian, et al. We think that this is very salutary and significant.

Though the assessments are still in draft form, we do know that every state using the CCSS will use either the Smarter Balanced or the Partnership for Assessment of Readiness for College and Careers (PARCC) assessment. We've been able to review draft test items, and it's safe to say that students are going to be asked to solve problems through reading and writing and to justify their solutions through reflection. Those test items, particularly the long and short performance items, make it abundantly clear that teaching kids information will no longer help them be successful on the tests. We believe that it was never the case that such teaching helped students be successful in life, so we applaud this shifting of the templates. To prepare students for success on the next generation of assessments and in life, a kind of sociocultural model of teaching called *inquiry* will have to hold sway.

Inquiry, as a term of art in cognitive science and as we use it in this book, is rigorous apprenticeship into expert thinking and problem solving. Inquiry requires knowledgeable teachers who create interesting and rewarding learning situations and who provide lots and lots of guided practice—the kind of practice that is focused like a laser on the development of real-world competence and expertise.

A final note on the CCSS: Lots of teachers we know think that the CCSS marginalize the teaching of narrative, especially literary narratives. We don't agree. The suggestion that students read and write mostly argument and informational texts in high school might make it look that way. But remember: Now every teacher across the curriculum is to teach reading and composing. This will leave English teachers the latitude to continue teaching lots of literature, but in ways that are complemented by their teaching of reading and writing literary nonfiction and other informational and argument texts. We explore ways of creating this kind of complementarity in the other books in our series (Smith, Wilhelm, and Fredricksen 2012; Wilhelm, Smith, and Fredricksen 2012). Inquiry is the ideal environment for rewarding the reading of literature in conversation with the reading and writing of other kinds of texts.

Finally, all three of us have devoted our professional lives to teaching young people to be more engaged and competent readers and composers. We have privileged the reading and writing of narrative as a unique and powerful way of knowing in our own teaching and in much of our professional work. This book is a continuation of that dedication to narrative as a way of knowing and transforming the self and the world. Even if there were no CCSS, we would teach according to the compelling principles that we'll be exploring throughout this book.

Toward Wide-Awake Teaching

Our goal in this book is to help all teachers—from the novice to the most experienced pro; from the teacher of language arts to all other disciplines found in schools; from the primary through the secondary grades—not to feel as though they are "strangers entering a strange land" when teaching strategies of narrative thinking and composing (Morgan 2003). Instead, we will outline the methods we use to help young people learn to compose (and read) narratives. These methods also offer a way to help students learn how to inquire into the ways stories shape and affect them and their communities. Dealing with uncertainty and difficult decisions, including decisions we make as teachers and writers every time we design instruction for our students, is nothing new (Floden and Clark 1988). We hope, though, to make our thinking visible to you so that you can teach with conscious competence. That is, we aim to share the principles we use to design instruction around narrative, and by extension, to share how we hope to build our students' narrative competency so that they can identify and inquire into the stories told about and around them.

More specifically, this book will address the following questions:

- What do I want my students to be able to do and understand as writers (and readers) of narratives?
- How can I design instruction that helps students compose narratives and helps them be able to inquire into the ways in which narratives work in the world?

Our Teaching Heuristics: Five Kinds of Composing and Five Kinds of Knowledge

When we think about our instructional design decisions, we work with two frameworks. These frameworks serve as teaching heuristics. In other words, they are generative frameworks for helping us plan our teaching, for solving problems on the fly during our teaching, and for reflecting and learning from our teaching so we can improve unit by unit and year by year. We call these frameworks the "five kinds of composing" and the "five kinds of knowledge."

The first framework is based on the idea that writers compose for different purposes at different times. In brief, expert writers compose for the following reasons as they work on real compositional problems and projects.

- **Composing to practice**—Writers compose to try out techniques, to explore ideas, and to consider different ways of approaching rhetorical challenges.

- **Composing to plan**—Writers compose to generate the content, to figure out why they are committed to a project, and to determine what they need to do to complete a project in a way that meets their purposes and goals.

- **Composing to create initial drafts**—Writers compose to move forward on a piece and to discover how their plans might change. We also refer to this as "early draft" composing.

- **Composing to create final drafts**—Writers compose to complete a project and to consider the needs of an audience.

- **Composing to transfer**—Writers compose to reflect, to look back at the choices they made when composing a piece, and to consider what they learned that could be used in future projects or in other contexts.

We want to be clear that the different kinds of composing are not about different kinds of projects, but are rather the different kinds of composing expert authors engage in during one project. We think this distinction matters when considering how we design and sequence our instruction, which we will make very clear in Chapters 5, 6, 7, and 8—the chapters that show example sequences of instruction.

The other framework that grounds our work comes from George Hillocks (1995), a mentor to all of us both through direct personal contact and through our reading of his publications. In brief, Hillocks argues that writers need to understand both the formal features of the texts they plan to compose and the content that will be central to those texts. And they need to be able to both name what they know (what educational psychologist call *declarative knowledge*) and perform what they know (what educational psychologist call *procedural knowledge*). The following chart provides a visual representation of these four kinds of knowledge. Jeff has dubbed this chart the *inquiry square* (see also Wilhelm, Baker, and Dube-Hackett 2001; Wilhelm 2001):

	Declarative Knowledge	Procedural Knowledge
Form	Understanding the features of a piece and how they are related to one another	Knowing how to create the features of a piece that help a reader recognize it as a specific kind of text
Substance	Understanding the concepts within a piece and how those concepts work together	Knowing how to go about gaining that conceptual understanding

But these types of knowledge don't exist in a vacuum. What one needs to know or do is a function of both one's context and one's purpose. In addition to the four kinds of knowledge described above, we also add another box that we are labeling the "Knowledge of Context and Purpose." Think about it: You likely have different purposes in telling a teaching story to, say, your principal than to your closest colleague. And you'd almost certainly tell it in a different way, from the content you'd include to the language you'd use to render that content. The inquiry square, then, might be better understood as a square within a square as in what follows:

	Declarative Knowledge	Procedural Knowledge
Form	Understanding the features of a piece and how they are related to one another	Knowing how to create the features of a piece that help a reader recognize it as a specific kind of text
Substance	Understanding the concepts within a piece and how those concepts work together	Knowing how to go about gaining that conceptual understanding
Knowledge of Context and Purpose: Understanding Where, When, and Why This Kind of Text Works in the World		

The importance of context and purpose makes it crucial for us to think about planning in terms of units instead of in terms of assignments. That is, when you have your students craft a particular kind of story (e.g., a fairy tale, a children's book, a digital story, a short story, a comic strip, etc.), the actual piece of writing that students create should be situated within a larger inquiry unit in which that piece of writing matters. Because students are engaged in a larger inquiry, they will already be reading about and discussing what others have to say about key concepts and the relationships between those concepts within a unit.

Of course, these two heuristics wouldn't be useful if they didn't complement each other. We think they do. For example, knowledge of purpose and context is developed through composing to plan. Procedural knowledge of substance—or knowing how to access and generate material as one reads and composes—is certainly part of composing to plan and practice. Procedural knowledge of form—or knowing how to shape what one is reading into a mental model or story world and knowing how to shape the gathered material for writing—is developed in composing to practice. As students learn to generate content, they learn to name that content and develop procedural knowledge of substance. Likewise, as they practice shaping that content, they necessarily learn to name that structuring that constitutes declarative knowledge of form. The *what* is learned best through the *how*.

As students go through the process of writing, they will further develop and consolidate the different kinds of knowledge as they draft, finalize, and polish their drafts, and ultimately as they reflect on the substance and process of their composing in composing to transfer. This kind of composing names what they have done and learned in ways that are amenable to transfer to future projects. This kind of composing, called *reflection* by the CCSS, is required on all the short and long performance tasks we have seen.

Figure 1.1 puts the five kinds of composing and the five kinds of knowledge together in a planning template that we have found useful. We want to highlight a few things about this template, which should be adapted and adjusted in a way that makes sense to you. One, we have placed the different kinds of composing as the headers of sections to help you see how the activities you sequence support students in particular kinds of composing. That is, you'll want to think about how an activity helps students compose in order to practice something or to plan something or to take an initial stab at a draft. Two, we have these different kinds

Figure 1.1 A Planning Template

1. Background for you to consider before students begin working through the sequence:
   - What overarching question for the unit is this sequence situated within?
   - What specific kind of story do you want your students to create?
   - What student-friendly prompt for the task of creating this product will your students receive from you?
     - What role do you want students to take as writers?
     - Who is the target audience for the piece?
     - What is the purpose of the piece?
     - What are the features of a strong, well-executed piece? (Wiggins and McTighe 2005)
2. What activities can you design and sequence to help students create a strong product and that help them understand what it is you want them to learn about narrative?

ACTIVITIES FOR COMPOSING TO PRACTICE	
Activities and Their Steps	*Evidence of Understanding (Parts of Inquiry Square) You Will Look for as Students Engage in These Activities*
Activity 1: (Name of activity here) • Steps for you and students to follow • Resources you might need Include any prompts and/or questions you want students to ask and/or answer during or as a result of this activity. (When working with students, you will have multiple activities for this kind of composing. Some of these activities might get after different kinds of knowledge.)	Procedural knowledge of substance (for example) In this box, identify not only *what kind of* knowledge, but also *how* the activity gets after this kind of knowledge.
ACTIVITIES FOR COMPOSING TO PLAN	
Activity 2: • Steps for you and students to follow • Resources you might need	Knowledge of purpose and context Procedural knowledge of form (for example)
ACTIVITIES FOR COMPOSING INITIAL DRAFTS	
Activity 3: • Steps for you and students to follow • Resources you might need	Declarative knowledge of form (for example)
ACTIVITIES FOR COMPOSING FINAL DRAFTS	
Activity 4: • Steps for you and students to follow • Resources you might need	Declarative knowledge of substance (for example)

(continues)

Figure 1.1   *Continued*

ACTIVITIES FOR COMPOSING TO TRANSFER	
Activity 5: • Steps for you and students to follow • Resources you might need	Knowledge of Purpose and Context (for example)
Please note: In each section the number of activities can vary, according to the teacher. For instance, you might want three activities for composing to plan in one unit and five activities in another unit.	

3. Reflective questions for you to consider about the sequence: *What* do you hope that creating this product through this sequence will help students understand about narrative and *how* does this sequence accomplish this instructional goal?

of composing in an order (to practice then to plan then to initiate a draft and so on). These purposes are interchangeable in some ways. For instance, Jeff likes to have his students compose to plan first, but Jim and Michael often have students begin by composing to practice. The important idea is that when writers compose an extended piece, they engage in the act of writing for different reasons, and as teachers, we aim to provide support for these varied reasons through a range of activities we engage in with our students. Three, the five kinds of knowledge (aka the inquiry square) guide our assessment of our students' understanding. When students engage in different activities to compose for any of the five different purposes (to practice, to plan, etc.), we want to pay attention to what students understand or can do. This means that sometimes when students compose to practice, we might be paying attention to their procedural knowledge of understanding a genre (procedural knowledge of form) and other times we might focus on their procedural knowledge of understanding the content of what they are writing (procedural knowledge of substance). In other words, the five kinds of composing are *not* a direct match with a particular piece of the five kinds of knowledge. As with any activity you do with your students, your assessment of student understanding could focus on a range of things.

The template in Figure 1.1 puts the kinds of composing (what students are doing) in relation to the kinds of knowledge (what teachers are paying attention to), because when we plan, we want to be clear about our purposes to guide our gaze when we are working with students.

The Organization of the Book

As you read *So, What's the Story? Teaching Narrative to Understand Ourselves, Others, and the World*, you will notice that Chapters 2 through 4 focus on the kinds of things that writers consider when composing stories. These chapters will first explore the five kinds of knowledge as related to narrative: knowledge of purpose and context (Chapter 2), procedural and declarative knowledge of substance (Chapter 3), and procedural and declarative knowledge of form (Chapter 4).

Chapters 5, 6, 7, and 8 show actual progressions of lessons about specific kinds of narratives in more detail, though we think the takeaway from these chapters is less about the actual activities and more about seeing our heuristics and principles in action. That is, we hope you will adapt the principles you see in our sequences for use with your students. We hope we are sparking a new way for you to think about creating more systematic sequences for your students, and like any instructional activity, we hope we can learn from you as you try things out with your students and as you learn from them in how they respond to what you try.

Our final chapter examines the idea of "service" in two ways. One, we want to consider how narrative services other kinds of thinking, like argument and description. Two, we want to consider how understanding narrative concepts can serve students as they investigate narratives. That is, we want our students to engage in narrative as a mode of inquiry as well as narrative as an object of inquiry, and we propose a few ways in which that might occur. Our logic can be described as moving from composing stories in order to understand and apply narrative principles, which in turn can make visible the ways in which narratives work individually and collectively in the world. Investigating narratives as objects of and as a mode of inquiry means that students can understand the ways in which the act of sharing a story changes how people view what might seem to be the stock stories of a community—that set of standard, typical stories that explain and maintain the status quo (Bell 2010).

Although we know you are likely facing the challenge and uncertainty of implementing the CCSS, we think this is a time and an opportunity for us to use the CCSS as leverage to do the work we have always believed is important for our students, namely becoming active, critical, and ethical participants in their communities. So although the CCSS anchor standard for narrative writing reads that students will "write narratives to develop real or imagined experiences or events using effective technique, well-chosen details, and well-structured event sequences," we think we can aid our students by helping them to see how making the leap from writing stories to understanding narrative can empower them and bring them, and you, hope.

It is important work that you do as you help students compose and understand narratives, and our hope is that the pages that follow offer you ways of thinking that trigger new and helpful ideas for you and your students. In the end, the story of you and your students should be one in which you see yourselves as empowered and hopeful too.

Why Narratives Matter

Knowledge of Purposes and Contexts

I decided to devote my life to telling the story
because I felt that having survived I owe something to the dead.
And anyone who does not remember betrays them again.

—**Elie Wiesel,** Holocaust survivor, Nobel Laureate, author

Why teach narrative? A big question to which we have a big (though simply stated) answer: Narratives help us live our lives, and they help us do our work.

Thinking About Purpose:
How Narratives Help Us Live Our Lives

Tracy, a seventh grader in Mrs. Rachel Ferguson's language arts class (pseudonyms), was one of those kids who kept to herself and didn't even talk much to her teacher. Tracy rarely, if ever, wrote much more than a paragraph, and she certainly wouldn't share. Then, sometime in May, she raised her hand.

"Mrs. Ferguson, would it be OK if I read my story?"

The class had been working on writing personal narratives, and Mrs. Ferguson was thrilled that Tracy wanted to read. The other kids in the class looked a little confused and curious. Some of them didn't even really know what Tracy's voice sounded like.

Tracy stood, her long black hair falling past her shoulders and her eyes staring at her story that she held in her hands. Then she began to read in her quiet, quivering voice.

She began with the line, "I heard thirteen shots, then silence." It was the story of hiding in her closet, listening to bullet after bullet. Then, when her stepdad slammed the door behind him, Tracy raced down the stairs and listened to her mom from the other side of the kitchen door.

"Don't come in here. Get help."

As Tracy finished her piece, she ended by saying that her mom was in the hospital and that when people would say to her that she was lucky, she would reply, "No. I am blessed."

A couple of months later, Mrs. Ferguson sat in a National Writing Project writing group and shared this story about Tracy. Mrs. Ferguson's story was not just about what happened to Tracy at home, but how Tracy's sharing of her story in the final weeks of the class had helped the classroom community to better understand Tracy. Over the course of the year, Mrs. Ferguson and the students read and wrote, sharing drafts and ideas with one another—in small groups, in whole-class discussions. The class got along just fine, but no one had taken the kind of personal risk in sharing like Tracy did. By sharing her story, Tracy transformed Mrs. Ferguson's classroom into a place of safety and stability for her. And when Mrs. Ferguson shared her teaching story of working with Tracy, she created a space for the Writing Project community to exchange stories and ideas that deepened the community's shared commitment to using writing as a vehicle to make their classrooms supportive places for all students, even the most reticent and troubled. The power of sharing stories lies in this kind of ripple effect between people and within their communities.

Both Tracy's sharing in her classroom and Mrs. Ferguson's sharing in her writing group illustrate the words of Dyson and Genishi (1994) when they write how storytelling can provide a way to understand ourselves, others, and our community. "The storytelling self is a social self," they write, "who declares and shapes important relationships through the mediating power of words. Thus, in sharing stories, we have the potential for forging new relationships, including local, classroom 'cultures' in which individuals are interconnected and new 'we's' formed" (5).

Fortunately, we don't have any stories that are quite so dramatic, but all of us have also experienced the power of stories. Several years ago when Jim's marriage suddenly ended, he sought counsel from a professional. It was a painful time, and he was nervous about talking to someone about his failed relationship. Moreover, seeing a counselor simply felt like a failure in some way. Despite these initial misgivings, this turned out to be one of the best things he ever did for himself and for the people in his life, who were quite unsure how to help him beyond being present for him.

The counselor, a joyful woman, welcomed Jim into her small office with wide-open arms. "Come on in," she said.

The room was small, and it felt like a comfortable living room at a friend's apartment. He sat in the oversized chair while she sat on the couch.

"So, why are we here?" she asked.

Jim told her about his wedding ceremony a few months before, about the inability for him and his new bride to talk about the hard stuff—about their uncertainty about how to solve problems together, and about their mutual decision to move on, independently of one another. It was a verbal dump.

The counselor looked at him, her hands sitting comfortably on her lap, her head nodding in that understanding and agreeing kind of way. "I want you to tell me something," she said. "I want you to tell me about how each of your romantic relationships in your life began and how they ended."

"Over my whole life?"

"It's up to you, but start at what you think is the beginning."

Jim began with high school and after describing three beginnings and three endings, he stopped. "I see the pattern. We don't have to go any farther if that's the point." From there Jim and the counselor were able to do substantial work into changing those patterns and in changing the way he approached the relationships in his life. Telling his story of relationships to a professional allowed both he and the counselor to look back at the past, to see patterns of behavior and thought. Moreover, articulating those patterns allowed him to imagine new ways of being, of thinking, and of feeling.

We see similar work being done by stories that are not personal or even real, but that are instead imagined. Let's take a look at a fictional short story that Jim wrote a while ago. We include it in Appendix A to refer to here and in later chapters. In the story we meet Mr. O'Conner, a lonely widower, and we meet Amanda, an injured teenager who is angry that her father left her and her mom a year ago. In the story, Mr. O'Conner and Amanda find themselves telling one another stories that seem to bring them to a closer understanding of who they each are independently and also how they might find comfort and a closeness with each other.

Although the story might need some more work (go ahead, by the way, and share it with your students as a piece to revise if you feel inclined), it is important to note the context in which Jim wrote and shared the piece in order to show how the story helped him in a new community. Several years ago, when Jim began his graduate studies he met weekly with a group of colleagues each week to discuss big ideas they were reading, to work through the transitions they each felt as they moved from full-time public school teachers to full-time graduate students, and to simply enjoy one another. Occasionally, members of the group would share something that they had written that had nothing to do with school. One person brought in a song he wrote. One person brought in poetry. Another brought a short story. And so on. Jim brought his story of Mr. O'Conner and Amanda. At a time of transition and a shift in professional identity, the story helped Jim identify himself as more than a graduate student, but also as a writer. It helped his new peers see what he valued and how he made sense of the world. Moreover, the exchange of pieces cemented the value the group placed on creating and on sharing. It helped the group recognize one another, not only as students in courses together but as people who were looking back and imagining what could or might be.

Michael and Jeff have experienced the power of story in many ways as well. A quick example from each: Michael and his wife Karen, both of whom are European American, have adopted two children of color. One of the best pieces of parenting advice they received was at a workshop in which the presenter stressed the importance of telling family stories both about generations past and the current generation. These stories, the presenter said, work to make kids feel they belong. So for the past two decades Michael and Karen have been doing just that. Over the years some of the stories have been told so much they become almost set pieces. One of the girls' favorites is about the time their dad took out a plate for his bagel and then put the plate and the bagel right back into the cabinet instead of taking it to the toaster. The story chronicles how Michael had the audacity to accuse someone of taking his food until he sheepishly had to withdraw his complaint because he found the bagel when he went to set the table for lunch. Lots of laughter has accompanied the telling of that story over the years. Michael claims that part of the laughter is a consequence of how the story has been embellished over the years so that now it's closer to fiction than it is to what actually happened. Catherine and Rachel, of course, disagree.

In Jeff's family, the value of story has achieved the status of a decision-making heuristic. Jeff heard a cowboy poet on NPR once say that Americans' obsession with materialism led to impoverished living. He maintained that the old bumper sticker: "He who dies with the most toys, wins" should be revised to "He who dies with the most stories, wins." Whenever the family or a family member has a decision to make, whether it is small or large, Jeff—or now one of his daughters—is likely to ask, "Which decision will give you the best story?" This past summer, Jazzy had the chance to take a well-paying job or to spend the first half of the summer in Italy studying art, and the second half on a Grand Canyon rafting trip. Jazzy is a conscientious girl, and hearing Jeff ask, "What will give you the best story?" freed her, she later said, to make the decision she had truly wanted to make anyway. During her trips she kept a journal, and she later recalled that when journaling she thought in terms of the stories she would want to tell family and friends when she returned from her trip—like the story of getting propelled out of her ducky on the Colorado River because she tried to punch through a big hole, or the time she was locked out of the Youth Hostel in Siena and thought she would have to sleep in a park.

As our examples illustrate, narratives help us understand and share where we come from. But it's crucially important to recognize that narratives help us set a trajectory for our futures and that they are especially important in helping us explore what is expected of us and how we might want to resist expectation. Jerome Bruner (2002) describes this resistance function of narrative well.

> We know that narrative in all its forms is a dialectic between what was expected and what came to pass. For there to be story, *something unforeseen must happen.* Story is enormously sensitive to whatever challenges our conception of the canonical. It is an instrument *not so much for solving problems as for finding them.* The plight depicted marks a story's type as much as the resolution. We more often tell stories to forewarn than to instruct. And because of this, stories are a culture's coin and currency. For culture is, figuratively, the maker and enforcer of

what is expected, but it also, paradoxically, compiles, even slyly treasures, transgressions, tilts myths and its folktales, its dramas and its pageants memorialize both its norms and notable violations of them. (15, italics added)

The stories Jim told with his counselor are helping him compose a new story of how he wants to relate to the people he loves. The stories Michael and his family tell help them write a new one about what it means to be a multiracial family. Jazzy's stories helped her see that money is not what matters and have helped her resolve to always be alert for opportunities that will enrich her life.

Thinking About Purpose: How Narratives Help Us Do Our Work

We see narrative empowering individuals as they negotiate the day-to-day experiences of their lives, but we also see an understanding of narrative as being essential for people in a whole host of careers and professions.

- Think of Click and Clack, the Tappet Brothers, whose *Car Talk* radio show each week on NPR is not only about fixing a particular car problem, but one in which they ask each caller to share where they live, how they drive, what they hear and notice, and so on. They use narrative concepts to tease out how things have been and to figure out what the break or trouble might be, and then they offer a new course of action or possibility—a kind of story of redemption following the story of the fall.

- Think of the residential Realtor who sees her job not as helping people sell or acquire property, but as someone who is helping her clients transition from one home to a new home, from one kind of story to another kind of story, from one way of living and expressing identity to another.

- Think of miners who, when sharing their stories to the technical writers charged with creating safety procedures, documents, and training, use not just their words but also their body language, which is vital to understanding their knowledge and expertise (Sauer 2003).

- Think of any kind of designer who can use stories during the design process, particularly when that process includes multiple team members (Danko, Meneely, and Portillo 2006). Stories can help show how ideas have developed and changed; stories can help the team create shared goals; stories can be used by insiders and outsiders of the design process to communicate ideas and to foster understanding (Erickson 1995).

- Think of lawyers as not just working with a case, but as dealing with a client in trouble. "And trouble," Bruner says in an interview, "is a narrative idea. You have to have trouble for there to be a story" (Charon 2006, 7). Storytelling can build juror empathy (Massaro 1989), and narratives can help people in the courtroom see different perspectives and to change the status quo (Delgado 1989).

- Think of bioethicists who use narratives as a "means to enhance understanding of the multiple values and conflicting perspectives at stake in medical action or inaction. It offers to situate moral thought within a form of understanding that finds stories as valuable, in their own way, as statistics. . . . Principles, it appears, are not enough" (Morris 2002, 206). Distinctions between story and plot can be helpful for bioethicists. "Story is the actual set of events," Chambers and Montgomery write, "while plot is the teller's particular arrangements of those events" (2002, 77). When an ethicist or any case-based worker (e.g., legal fact-finding, medical diagnosis, criminal detection, teachers) seeks to understand what happened in a situation, "versions may conflict; the parties may invoke different values; individual interpreters may allege the importance of details that others discount or ignore" (78).

- Think of health professionals, such as doctors and nurses, who practice narrative medicine. "Narrative medicine," Rita Charon (2006), a medical doctor who has a Ph.D. in literature, writes, "makes the case that narrative training in reading and writing contributes to clinical effectiveness. By developing narrative competence, we have argued, health care professionals can become more attentive to patients, more attuned to patients' experiences, more reflective in their own practice, and more accurate in interpreting stories patients tell of illness" (107). Knowing and applying narrative concepts helps health professionals be "attuned to illness time" (121). Moreover, Charon writes about teams of health professionals who share their stories with one another, which also helps create a sense of community. "I reach my colleagues and teammates more systematically and personally and consequentially by virtue of hearing what they write about their clinical work and their hearing what I write about mine. All of us who read and write in clinical settings are finding that our practices build community . . . Our shared narrative acts enable us to affiliate into effective dyads of care with individual patients and into cohesive professional collective with colleagues" (2006, 150).

What each of these (and other practice-based, human professions) share is the idea that narrative understanding can help people make sense of what they expected, what went awry or broke that expectation, and what they might see as new possibilities. Narrative understanding can help foster a new understanding of self and of others, and it can also help people solve real problems together. In short, understanding narrative empowers people.

As the stories we shared above indicate, we see the purpose of narrating as being vitally important in helping students become "college and career ready," the fundamental goal of the Common Core State Standards (CCSS), but we also believe that knowing how to compose and how to read narratives is something that matters to people in their lives beyond college and beyond careers. We see narrative as a way for people to understand themselves, others, and the communities in which they participate.

Thinking About Context

Of course, none of the stories we have written about were composed in a vacuum. Rymes (2009) helps us understand how both the immediate and the larger surrounding context shape the stories we compose. In her work Rymes highlights the importance of both the interactional context and the social contexts. The interactional context includes what happens between the teller and the audience during the storytelling occasion, such as what happened between Jim and his counselor or between Michael and his family members. It is important to pay attention to the interactional context because doing so helps tellers and audiences know what to expect in an interaction (e.g., when to answer a question; when to accept an invitation; etc.) and to know when those expectations are foiled (e.g., when an audience responds with silence instead of an expected response like laughter).

The social contextual features, according to Rymes (2009), are those broad influences outside of the interaction that influence what happens within the interaction. These outside influences might be things like gender expectations, institutional expectations, race, family, socioeconomic influences, and so on. We also point to social contexts to demonstrate how the story within an interaction can reflect those outside influences, and how potentially, those stories could resist or challenge and even change those outside influences. For instance, in Jim's exchange with his counselor outside influences might have included his relationships with his family, his expectations of what constitutes a healthy relationship, his Catholic upbringing, his middle-classness, and surely more. Working through his story with his counselor not only allowed him to understand himself better, but he also began to see how some of those outside influences affected how he told and understood his story. Moreover, it changed how he began to see the boundaries and expectations of someone involved in the kind of healthy relationship he seeks—in the stories he wants to tell and live out in his future.

As much as we endorse the CCSS' call in writing anchor standard 3 that students should "write narratives to develop real or imagined experiences or events using effective technique, well-chosen details, and well-structured event sequences" (18), Rymes' work has helped us understand that more is at stake. We need to move beyond the CCSS, because if we only stick with the standards, we focus only on the crafting of individual stories, rather than on how those stories might operate in communities. We think this is limiting, because it can keep students' focus only on the schoolishness of a task, rather than on the wider purposes, principles, and contexts of narratives. Exceeding the CCSS, we believe, will make both the CCSS and narrative matter more to students.

That is, we don't want our students to only write stories because we assign them; instead, we want our students to compose stories because stories are vital to the ways in which people and communities understand themselves. Put more simply, we want students to write stories in order to be empowered to participate in their communities.

Making narrative discourses visible to students can help them not only read the word or read the world, but also see how the word is written by the world and how the world is written by the word. Making the work of narratives visible to our students, we believe, can help them see the way things (might) have been and the way things might be. As Bruner writes, "Through narrative, we construct, reconstruct, in some ways, reinvent yesterday and tomorrow. Memory and imagination fuse in the process" (2002, 93). We need to help our students understand how this happens.

Implications for Planning and Practice

We'll be sharing lots of specific ideas for instruction throughout the book, but as we close this chapter, we offer a few activities you might try with your students to help them identify the purposes of and the contexts within which stories appear.

1. Have students listen to the stories shared in their communities (e.g., family, school, work, neighborhood, clubs, teams, etc.). Ask them to identify a particular story someone shares in order to see what that story suggests about the values, relationships, emotions, identities, and so on that are important to that community.

2. Have students look at stories within pop culture (e.g., movies, songs, television shows, video games, etc.). Have them identify the teller and the audiences, as well as some of the social contexts that might be informed by the story and/or that might inform the story being shared through the pop culture artifact.

3. Have students examine humor, particularly jokes, because part of what makes humor work is that there is a gap between what is expected to be shared and what the humorist actually shares (Vorhaus 1994). Ask students to consider what an audience had to expect and what the storyteller did in the piece to create a gap. What does that gap reveal about what the community finds important? Or if the student rejects the joke as racist or sexist or just not funny, what values are expressed by the audience's response?

4. Have students examine the stories presented on a nightly newscast or in a newspaper or magazine or on a website. What patterns do they see with how particular kinds of people are presented? What does the storyteller seem to think is important for the audience? What does that reveal about what the storyteller thinks the community values or wants them to value? How are audience members positioned in relationship to the subjects of the stories and how are the storytellers positioned?

The idea behind these activities is to help students identify the assumptions the storytellers and the audiences share because identifying them can help students see the purpose and the context of the stories being told. We can sum up our thinking here with two guiding questions:

- What assumptions are at play in the story itself and how can these assumptions be applied to our lives; for example, what happens to the character we follow, and why does this happen? What are we supposed to think about the character? What are we supposed to learn from what happens to the character?
- What assumptions are at play in the exchange between the storyteller and the audience?

In answering these questions, students will be developing the knowledge of purpose and context and so will pave the way for their developing the other four types of knowledge that they need. In so doing, they will be working toward achieving CCSS anchor writing standard 3. By casting students as ethnographers of story in their communities and culture, they will also be working toward achieving the CCSS anchor reading standards associated with craft and structure (4–6) and the writing standards associate with research, especially 6 and 7. But students will also be doing more than working toward the standards. They will be well on their way to exceeding the CCSS by understanding narrative as a unique and powerful way of personal knowing, of professional ways of understanding others, and of undertaking communal action.

CHAPTER 3

Thinking About the Substance of Stories

I find that most people know what a story is
until they sit down to write one.

—Flannery O'Connor

In our previous chapter, we shared quite a few stories. And although those stories were different, they shared some fundamental features. These features are outlined by Jerome Bruner (1991), though we've translated his terminology to help us in our work with young people. The features are important because they remind us what to keep in mind as we teach, what it is we need to do to help students become better writers (and readers) of narratives.

We'll first look at Bruner's narrative principles in action through Tracy's story of her stepfather's attack on her mother that we presented in the previous chapter. It's so dramatic that we're sure you'll remember it. Then we will elaborate on these principles and share some ideas about how we can help students enact them.

How Stories Work

In the first place, Tracy's story highlights the idea that *a story depends on a break in what was expected*, an idea we introduced in the previous chapter. Bruner labels this as "canonicity and breach." Tracy's story challenges our expectation that young people should live in homes of safety and stability. Tracy's story didn't continue to the aftermath of the attack, but because of Rachel Ferguson's teaching story, we do know that after Tracy told it she began exhibiting a change in her actions and potentially in her values. Bruner refers to this as "intentional state entailment," that is, the principle that *a story shows changes in characters, especially in their understanding, values, or intentional actions.*

Stories play out on these two levels of action and awareness, which Bruner (1986) refers to as the "landscape of action" and the "landscape of consciousness." He points out that storytellers have to work on these two landscapes simultaneously, which makes storytelling a challenge because storytellers have to share not only what happens, but also how characters make sense of the events they encounter and how they may be changed or transformed by these events.

This focus on action and awareness points to another move that all stories make, which is that they each include a filter and a slant. By *filter,* we mean that the audience follows a particular character or person. Tracy's story, for example, focused on herself and not her mother or stepfather. By *slant,* we mean that the story takes a particular attitude toward the experiences the character or people have. Tracy makes it clear that she is resolved not to let the horrible event crush her.

The fact that a story has both a filter and a slant leads to two more narrative principles. First, *a story is open to interpretation by not always being explicit about what it means,* what Bruner calls "hermeneutic composability." We might wonder what it says about Tracy that she pledged to persevere or whether it takes such a dramatic classroom event to result in the changes that Rachel detailed in her teaching story. Second, *a story invites more questions than it poses solutions,* what Bruner calls "normativeness." Because the storyteller employs a character to filter the audience's experience and has an attitude toward that character's experience, the audience is permitted and even expected to be active interpreters and to ask questions about what characters do and about how characters make sense of that experience and also what they might have done in a similar circumstance. We might wonder, for example, what happened to Tracy's mother or think about what we would have done had one of our students shared a similar story.

The audiences for stories also rely on the storyteller to make choices about the storyworld and about the boundaries where a story begins and ends. That is, *a story adheres to the rules it creates for itself.* A storyteller presents a world that establishes its own rules (e.g., a fantasy story, a science fiction story, a realistic story, etc.). Bruner labels this as "referentiality." A storyteller also must put boundaries around time, which means that a storyteller decides when to begin and to end the events or sequence of events revealed to an audience. That is, *a story shapes time*. Bruner calls this "narrative diachronicity." It does so because *a story focuses on a particular event or series of events* (i.e., Bruner's "particularity"). Tracy does not provide much background at the beginning of her narrative; instead, she decides to begin at the moment when she heard shots fired, and she ends by letting the audience know that her mom lived and that she expected and planned to have a different kind of experience this summer. Tracy's story adheres to the rules of the world she presents (a realistic world) when she does not have a spaceship drop into the scene or have someone with superhero powers magically make things better.

Finally, as we point out in Chapters 1 and 2, all stories appear in particular contexts, so we take into account some of the narrative principles that speak to the purposes and contexts of stories. Or, rather, these principles speak to the implicit agreement between a storyteller and an audience. One, *a story is recognizable and understandable in form*. That is, an audience recognizes the particular kind of story it is. Bruner refers to this as the "genericness" of stories, and when Tracy shares her story with her classmates, she applies what she and her classmates have learned as features of personal narratives, namely that it should include details about a pivotal event and details about how that experience shaped their thinking or feelings.

Two, storytellers and audiences rely on what Bruner refers to as "narrative accrual." That is, *a story builds on and is connected to other stories*. Tracy's audience likely considered other stories about home life, about the relationship between parents, about their own experiences (if any) with tragedies, and even about their own experiences with Tracy.

Three, storytellers must also grapple with an audience's background knowledge, as well as with their own intentions for the story. *A story is shared for a reason and relies on the background knowledge of an audience* (Bruner's "context sensitivity and negotiability"). We know that when telling stories to different audiences, we may have to adjust the details in order to help us shape the audience's experience. For example, when Rachel told her colleagues about Tracy's story, she had to include details about her school, about the typical kind of student in her classroom, and about Tracy's position within her classroom. This is likely different than the kind of details she had to supply to her teaching partner down the hallway at her school on the day when Tracy shared her story.

The following chart summarizes these principles:

Bruner's Terms	How We See the Features as Narrative Principles	The Substance of Stories
Canonicity and breach	A story highlights a break in what was supposed to be or what was expected to be.	Character
Intentional state entailment	A story shows changes in characters, especially in their values or in their intentional actions.	
Hermeneutic composability	A story is open to interpretation by not always being explicit about what it means.	Filter and slant
Normativeness	A story invites more questions than it poses solutions.	
Referentiality	A story adheres to the rules it creates for its storyworld.	Storyworld
Narrative diachronicity	A story shapes time.	Time
Particularity	A story focuses on a particular event or series of events.	
Genericness	A story is recognizable and understandable in form.	Purpose and context (implicit understanding between the audience and the storyteller)
Narrative accrual	A story builds on and is connected to other stories.	
Context sensitivity and negotiability	A story is shared for a reason and relies on the background knowledge of an audience.	

These principles help us see what storytellers have to create or choose when they begin to compose a story. And they are borne out in the writing writers do about their craft.

Developing Procedural Knowledge of Substance

Creating Compelling Characters

Ray Bradbury once said, "My characters write my stories for me. They tell me what they want, and I tell them to go get it, and I follow as they run, working at my typing as they rush to their destiny" (Koch 2003, 15). Bradbury makes this process sound easy, but we know that having our students compose believable characters and write compelling stories for them can be difficult. This difficulty is often the result of students paying more attention to action and less attention to what Bradbury is suggesting, namely that stories are about finding what a character desires and following the character as she pursues it.

Kurt Vonnegut also believes that the entry into story is through character motivation. "It's the writer's job to stage confrontations," Vonnegut said, "so the characters will say surprising and revealing things, and educate and entertain us all" (Koch 2003, 15). Pulitzer Prize–winning journalist Jon Franklin agrees: "The writer's goal is to understand how the character looks at the world and understand the character's responses to events" (Kramer, Call, and Harvard University Nieman Foundation for Journalism 2007, 128). Taken together, these writers make the case that authors are tasked with creating characters who want something, who believe that something is important, and who face confrontations in the pursuit of reaching what they want. So, how do storytellers create characters who have a strong and important desire that is worth pursuing?

John Truby (2007) offers ideas on how storytellers might create characters who, as Bruner suggests, experience changes, particularly changes in values. Truby writes, "Don't think of your main character as a fixed, complete person whom you then tell a story about. You must think of your hero as a range of change, a range of possibilities, from the very beginning. You have to determine the range of change of the hero at the start of the writing process, or change will be impossible for the hero at the end of the story" (2007, 79). The "range of change" Truby mentions is helpful in thinking about the protagonist of the story because the hero is the one who drives the action. A real and true change, according to Truby, is one in which the character's basic understandings/beliefs/values are challenged and changed. Mr. O'Conner, the protagonist in Jim's story in Appendix A, experiences the possibility of change when he connects to Amanda at the end of the story.

Some common ways, according to Truby, in which characters change include the following:

- child → adult
- participant → leader
- leader → cynic
- tyrant → leader
- metamorphosis (actually take on another life-form, like in some horror, fantasy, or fairy tales; or, even profound spiritual or psychic transformations).

Notice how each change involves a change in roles, which in turn, can create or express the possibility for a change in values. When a storyteller is presenting a range of change for the hero of a story, we see the humanity and flaws of the character. John Vorhaus (1994), author of *The Comic Toolbox: How to Be Funny Even If You're Not*, writes that it is the humanity of the character that helps the audience to connect with the character. It is this humanity that allows the audience to have sympathy and even empathy for the character. Dramatizing the strengths and flaws of the character helps to show how the character might be similar to or slightly different than the audience. In other words, the audience can see that the character is not simply a stock character, but rather one with a unique collection of traits, one that is worthy of our attention and care.

These character traits could be physical, social, emotional, experiential, and/or intellectual. It is this collection of traits—this humanity—that makes surprise and change possible for the character in the story and for the audience of the story. As author Brett Anthony Johnston (2007) writes, "To forge a relationship between your characters and your readers, focus on what makes a character vulnerable, focus on their inconsistencies, focus on their flawed humanity. This is of the utmost importance" (69).

We pause here to note that the imaginary character or the real person may have a desire that she feels is important enough to pursue regardless—and maybe despite—the obstacles facing her. When we write here of creating characters who have the possibility for change, especially of a change in values, we note that often the character is not aware that this change is needed or even possible—the character might even actively resist the necessary changes. However, pursuing the goal creates opportunities for that change to become possible. If we consider Jim's story of Amanda and Mr. O'Conner that we share in Appendix A, we can see that Amanda wanted to feel connected to her father, to hear his voice in her ear again. Perhaps she will reach out to him and in doing so she might grow as a person, moving from a young person to an adult, from someone who is not at peace with the relationship to someone who is more at peace with it. We don't know for sure, because in this story we only see her as feeling uncertain and grappling to come to terms with things as she shares her story with Mr. O'Conner.

When creating characters with a strong enough desire to pursue a goal that is worth facing obstacles for, characters who have a desire that involves the possibility of change, it helps to create contexts in which that character is able to come into contact with other characters—characters who might assist, resist, provide models of possibility or difficulty for the character who is the filter. That is, by creating a strong desire and high stakes for a character to pursue, storytellers can place the character on paths that overlap with those of other characters and people. All stories offer possibilities for using different character types, and those different types suggest particular relationships between characters, and these in turn suggest particular possibilities, meanings, and themes. Truby (2007) offers some typical character types, which in turn suggests how characters might be related to one another:

- hero
- opponent
- ally
- fake ally
- love interest
- buddy
- king or father
- queen or mother
- mentor
- warrior/protector
- magician/helper or deceiver
- rebel/with or against protagonist
- clown/trickster/fool/helper or deceiver.

These possible roles for characters to play can aid storytellers in discovering what possible changes a character might undergo. Oftentimes, we think these changes might be in what a character values. At the same time, these roles can also help storytellers figure out the nature of the relationship characters might have with others. Put another way, when storytellers begin to figure out roles that characters might play when they relate to others, the values and desires are dramatized, which makes for a more compelling story for an audience.

For instance, a hero's values are always in conflict with some other characters' values. These competing values are often behind the conflict that faces the hero of the story. Larry Brooks (2011) writes, "Conflict is something that opposes the goal you've given to your protagonist. Without conflict, the character is not required to summon courage or to conquer his own demons. Without conflict, life is easy, and that's not the stuff of a compelling story" (56). Notice here that we are focusing not on conflict for the sake of conflict, but on how conflict is a way to help the audience come to better understand the characters. The focus on the relationship between characters by what they value speaks directly to the characters' motivations.

For storytellers, the focus on characters' desires and values, the possibility of change in the character, and the relationships that exist among characters can help to generate and develop story ideas. Indeed, Stephen Koch (2003) writes that when a writer is developing a story and the story becomes disorganized, it is better to focus less on plot and much more on characters. In particular, Koch recommends focusing on the character whose fate matters most to the story: Ask yourself, "What does the character want?" and "Is the character going to get it? If yes, how, and if no, why?" (2003, 77). This set of questions helps us see how tellers of stories, in the early stages of their composing process, can simply practice and play with characters. That is, early on (and sometimes later on) in the process of writing a story, it is important for writers to invent or find many possible characters (or to consider the different desires or values that might be motivating people), because each one has her own story: her own desires, goals, values, relationships. Stories are everywhere in all the people and characters we meet and discover.

OK, we've spent a lot of time fleshing out how characters work in stories. Now let's turn to think about how we can help students create them. Peter Rubie and Gary Provost (1998) share a set of questions that we find especially useful. We call it the WAGS heuristic:

W—world of the character: Where does this character spend a lot of time? How does that world affect the character and how does the character affect that world?

A—action of the character: What does the character do during a regular day (routine actions)? What does the character do in pursuit of the goal shown in this story (exceptional actions)?

G—goal of the character: What does the character want? What does the character need (this is often different from the character's goal)?

S—stakes of the goal to the character: What bad thing does the character think will happen if the goal is not reached? What makes the goal worth pursuing and grappling with the obstacles and confrontations put in the way of attaining that goal?

The WAGS test focuses on desire and values and what motivates a character's actions. To illustrate the power of the heuristic, let's use it to look at Jim's character Amanda (see Appendix A):

W—She spends a lot of time at home alone and a lot of time with her basketball team.

A—She shoots hoops in the driveway; she supports her team.

G—She wants to be part of something and at peace with her dad being gone.

S—She knows being at peace means she will be less sad, less angry.

The desires of a character are easier to dramatize if those desires are specific. For example, using the WAGS heuristic would lead to including the quiet conversation Amanda had with Mr. O'Conner because it seems to provide her with a small sense of peace—if even momentarily—because she is remembering a particular memory with her father.

Once students are familiar with the WAGS heuristic, you can use it with them in a variety of ways. To prepare to write a story of their own (composing to practice), students can use the WAGS test for people they see in images. One thing we know about images, like photographs, paintings, posters, and so on, is that they imply stories rather than guide an audience through a story. We can use this to our advantage by having students use the WAGS test for characters in such images.

If students have already begun their narratives, they can use the WAGS heuristic to help them develop it (composing to plan). For example, they could use the WAGS heuristic for creating characters who might fit different roles (e.g., trickster, mentor, hero, love interest, etc.) in a character's community. Or they could use the WAGS heuristic for creating different characters who might have the same goals as their protagonist. For instance, a range of characters might want to be in the starting lineup of a basketball team. Or, a range of characters each might want to find love. You might create a range of goals and then have students create characters who each want to attain the same goal.

One challenge for students in writing about real people, especially people they know well, is that it's difficult to decide what to include and what to leave out. We think the WAGS test can help students choose and focus on the story they want to share through characters:

- Students can use the WAGS heuristic for people in their lives. You might have students write a long list of all the people they know or see or have met. Then, you can have them use the WAGS test to speculate what a person might want or what a person might see as important. Doing so can help students figure out a particular event or sequence of events that helps them dramatize that person's pursuit of that goal.

- Students can use the WAGS heuristic for people who engage in a typical event (e.g., weddings, first days of school, first bus/plane/car ride, falling short during a game or audition, etc.). Students might decide that these typical events are the beginning, middle, or end of a story, but the events can serve as a trigger to help students tell a story that people face.

- Students can use the WAGS heuristic for historical or famous people.

- Students can use the WAGS heuristic for significant relational characters for different stages of life (e.g., going to school, first dates, work, getting married/divorced, near death, etc.).

Each of these activities can be either composing to practice or composing to plan depending on whether the students will be making use of the work they did in composing subsequent narratives.

Creating Engaging Filters and Slants

The terms *filter* and *slant* derive from Seymour Chatman's (1990) *Coming to Terms: The Rhetoric of Narrative in Fiction and Film*. As we explained earlier in this chapter, *filter* is Chatman's term "for the perspectival bias, or vantage point, of a character in the storyworld as opposed to the attitudes of a narrator reporting events from a position outside that world" (Herman, McHale, and Phelan 2010, 301). *Slant* is Chatman's term "for the dispositions and attitudes of a narrator reporting events from a position outside the storyworld, as opposed to the perspectival bias or vantage point of a character in that narrated world" (Herman, McHale, and Phelan 2010, 312). These two terms, *filter* and *slant*, can help writers generate attitudes for characters toward the events and relationships they are experiencing in a story. We have found these concepts generative and helpful to students when they are composing, as well as when analyzing stories that they are reading.

Of course, these concepts are not only helpful in looking at fiction (e.g., novels, fairy tales, comic strips, etc.), but also in looking at nonfiction (e.g., biographies, memoirs, news stories, etc.). That is, the concepts of filter and slant can help students to read as writers as they figure out the moves the writers made in order to create filters and slants. For instance, the audience of stories might ask the following:

- Is the narrator trustworthy and credible? (See Smith 1991 and Smith and Wilhelm 2006 for sequences on teaching students how to judge narrator reliability.)
- Is the main character's slant allowing the writer to express what is essential, and as a reader to see all that I need to see? What is missing or withheld because of the particular slant?
- What does the storyteller's choice of a filter and slant have to say about what the storyteller wants me to notice and believe about the way things ought to be?
- What do I have to believe in order to agree or disagree with the storyteller? With the narrator? With the main character? Do I want to believe this or do I want to resist?

As a storyteller, one has to create and make a decision about the filter and slant a story offers. What kind of attitude toward people, places, time, and events will the filter character display? Will the filter character serve as the narrator? If not, what kind of attitude toward the filter character will the narrator have?

Various activities give students practice effectively making use of both filter and slant:

- Students could write about one scene from the different involved characters' points of view. You might have students act out a scene or a typical moment (e.g., say a car ride with friends or an argument with parents) and then have them write about what each character might be thinking and feeling about the occasion. What does each character notice? What is the emotional reaction and charge of each character? Why? What does each character think about things during the scene and afterward? What does the character want to change? What does the character want from the other character that the other character doesn't want to give up?

■ Students could write about an event filtered through the slants of people who have just experienced something. For instance, have students write about a car accident they just witnessed. First, filter it through a character who just lost a friend in a car accident. Second, have students filter the scene through a character who just won the lottery. Third, have students filter the scene though a character who just had a stranger buy her coffee just because. Fourth, have students filter the scene through a character who just broke up with a significant other. And so on. The idea here is to help students practice crafting and changing details that help an audience see the events through particular attitudes and emotions that characters bring to an event.

■ Students could write with different emotions. [*Creating Character Emotions* by Ann Hood (1998) is a helpful resource.] Have students create characters who experience an intense emotion (jealousy, fear, joy, etc.) as they describe a static setting (e.g., a city park, a barn, the inside of a public bus, a restaurant, etc.).

■ Students could write about a combination of emotions (what a character feels in a scene) and of attitudes (of a person narrating the scene). This might be best done first by students acting out a scene. The teacher provides a stimulus or scenario. Then the teacher provides each student with a note card designating a different emotion or roles that imply different emotions.

For instance, set the stage by having the characters in a small, confined space (e.g., a car, an elevator, a dinner table) with a situation in which the characters each want something different (e.g., family members responding to a mother's suggestion that the winter holiday be spent at her parents' house). Then, give each character a different emotion. After the scene is acted out, have each student write about what happened through the filter of one of the characters and with the attitude on the note card that each student holds.

- Students can report about an incident as though they are newscasters with different slants. The easiest example of this might be to play the recording of different sports teams' announcers broadcasting an important play in a game. One set of announcers will likely be thrilled; the others are likely to be dejected. Each set of announcers will likely filter the events through one player on his or her team, and the other set of announcers will filter it through a player on the other team. Have students report on events they might experience, such as sporting events, auditions, playground, family life, friend life, the lunchroom, and so on.

  Of course this can also be done regarding current events or political situations from the perspective of newscasters from different political ideologies, say Fox News and MSNBC. Such an activity has the added benefit of alerting students to different political perspectives and how these affect what news is reported and how it is reported upon.

After students have done any or all of this writing, it's important to share. For example, after students worked on the first activity we explained, they could meet in small groups with other students who employed the same filter. Students could do a read-around and then discuss how their renditions of the event are similar or different. Then groups can jigsaw and after another read-around discuss what filter is most effective for achieving what purpose. The possibilities for talk are virtually endless. What's important in whatever alternative you choose is that students have a chance to develop an articulated understanding of what they did and why they did it. Such an understanding is crucial for fostering transfer.

Creating a Storyworld

Creating characters, though necessary to creating a compelling story, is not always easy for every writer, nor the easiest place to begin. For some writers, a storyworld is an easier or more compelling place to begin. At any rate, creating a storyworld is necessary to creating narratives.

Although the word *storyworld* conjures up a particular setting of a story, here we refer to *storyworld* as narrative theorists define it: "the world evoked by a narrative text or discourse; a global mental model of the situations and events being recounted" (Herman, McHale, and Phelan 2010, 313). By using this definition, we highlight not only the time and place of the story, but also how the world operates, or its "referentiality" for audiences as Bruner might refer to it. It is not enough, for instance, for us to have known the place called Hogwarts where Harry Potter went to school; we need to also understand how things work in that world. The rules of the storyworld lead to characters who are faced with a set of constraints, connections between people, and opportunities (Smith and Wilhelm 2010). That is, storyworlds create boundaries and possibilities for characters to take action and to start, cultivate, and even end relationships. Storyworlds help shape characters, and characters shape storyworlds—much like we see stories shaping communities and communities shaping stories.

Jim used to teach at a middle school in a neighborhood where many of the students did not live. One activity he used to do with his students was to head out of the school and take a walk down the block to a park that had a good, wide view of many homes in the neighborhood. Jim asked his students to spread out and find a home with which they were unfamiliar; one that seemed interesting or different or curious to them. Then, he asked them to jot down as many physical details they noticed without judgment or evaluation. Rusty mailbox. Unclipped bushes. Tricycle and toys laying in the front yard. Cracked white paint on the garage door. And the like. After students had a long list of concrete physical details, then they had to ask themselves, based on this list, who do they think lives there? What do those people have as goals? What makes them restless, and how do they deal with their restlessness? After students wrote for a bit, everyone headed back to the classroom, and they posted the list of details of the homes on the wall. Students then had to pick a couple of other homes and, based on the details on the sheets they saw posted, they created more characters. Some characters owned or rented the homes. Some were kids or elderly. Some married or single. All had desires.

This exercise is much like Stephen Koch's (2003) advice for writers who begin with places as triggers for story ideas. Ask, "Who lives here? Who wants to visit here? Who wants to leave here? Why?" (78). The general idea is that characters are situated in their own slice of the world, and a context can often be a starting place to inventing a character and to finding a story idea. Similarly, when writing about real people, storytellers have to select the details about the storyworld. We think it is helpful for writers to select details that reveal something about the connection between the person and the boundaries and opportunities the storyworld presents to the person. For example, when Tracy shared her story about her stepfather and mother, she included details about her closet, about the doors that separated her from her mother, about the way time moved too slowly and too quickly at different moments, and so on. These details reveal how Tracy was affected by the constraints of the physical and psychological space in which she found herself.

In addition to a storyteller showing how a storyworld shapes the character's experience and action, a storyteller must also consider the storyworld in terms of the audience's experience. Ralph Fletcher (1993) writes about the advice John Gardner gives in creating this kind of connection between the character → the storyworld → the audience. In *The Art of Fiction*, John Gardner (1985) describes "good writing" as that which is "a vivid and continuous dream," Fletcher responds by writing, "This is a useful definition for all kinds of writing: bad writing is anything that jolts the reader out of that dream. The reader must make a leap of the imagination to connect his world to the world of the writer. The writer who can create a believable world, a convincing place, goes a long way toward trancing the reader into the larger world of the article, biography, poem, or story" (1993, 114).

One way for storytellers to create believable and convincing worlds is to be specific about natural spaces, about man-made settings, about cultural and historical references, and about the use and placement of objects and tools that characters interact with during the story. "Setting is where many writers get lost in chunks of narrative summary because it's easy, and even fun, to describe the setting," writes Jordan Rosenfeld (2008), the author of *Make a Scene*. "It's crucial to remember that setting exists mostly to serve as a way of both creating authenticity and grounding the reader in the scene (and story) at hand. If setting begins to take too much precedence, and distracts from your characters or storyline, then it needs to be tamed back" (50).

In the next chapter, we look at how storytellers might use description and action to show how a storyworld can help tell the character's story. For now, though, when creating characters and generating storyworlds, it is helpful to consider how a character shapes and is shaped by the world of the story. This can happen, in large part, by having the character interact with those natural spaces, man-made settings, and objects that are a part of the storyworld. That is, storytellers can show an audience how characters (or people) are shaped by the space and place they populate. Storytellers can show how the environment creates constraints, connections, and opportunities for characters (Smith and Wilhelm 2010).

Other possibilities for helping students learn how to develop storyworlds (composing to practice) abound:

- Students could create a map (or other kind of visual) or find a drawing or photo of a space they want to populate with characters (or of the place a real-life person inhabits). This might be a big, broad area (like in a science fiction story that takes characters around an entire galaxy), or it might be just a few blocks or even a room (like in Jim's story about Mr. O'Conner and Amanda). Drawing the space can help students see the various objects or landmarks that a character or person might interact with during a story. Students can ask of the world they draw: Who wants to be here? Who wants to leave here? What's keeping them here (or away)? Who else might someone meet in this space? And so on.

- Students could create a list of "rules" that people in the space might already know (or might need to learn). For example, in the movie *Pleasantville* the characters who populate the town know only that things work a particular way, but when brother and sister outsiders come to the town, the people of Pleasantville see new ways of being in relationship with one another. In the town of Pleasantville, the residents only see things in black and white (quite literally) and then when color is introduced, whole new opportunities and ways of thinking open up for characters (especially for one diner owner who begins to paint). Have students create their own rules for a town, and then have them write to see who would want to be in that space and who would want to leave that place. Or, have them bring in an outsider who shakes things up. The poet Richard Hugo (1979) calls these rules "triggers" for ideas for narrative poems—for example, imagine a town with only one person who works the second shift; imagine a town where everyone knows each other's name; imagine a town where "Each Sunday, a little after 4 P.M., the sky turns a depressing gray and the air becomes chilly" (20).

- Have students work with images of places. You might have them work with magazine photos, websites, real estate photos, paintings, and so on. The images can act as triggers for different constraints, connections, or opportunities for characters.
- Students might write classified ads for selling the objects that fill the space of a setting. Who might want to purchase the objects? Who wants to get rid of them? Why? What happens when the people meet?

Once again, after students have done this composing, it's crucially important for them to talk about it so they can reflect on what they did, how they'll make use of it in the narrative on which they are working, and how they will use what they learned in the future. Composing to practice becomes composing to plan and then composing to transfer.

Creating a Focus with Time-Related Choices

When we think of time related to story and storytelling, we consider both the internal time sequence (the duration of the sequence of events within a story) and the external time sequence (the duration of the presentation of the novel, play, story, etc.). Bruner (1991) describes one of the features of narrative, that it shapes time: It puts boundaries around time. Seymour Chatman (1990) explains this a bit more when he writes about *time being the distinguishing logic of narratives*. Whereas argument, for instance, operates on the validity of propositions, narrative is unique because it deals with time—with a chrono-logic. That is, storytellers decide which events to share with an audience, how to share that time with an audience (e.g., speed up long stretches of time in a few words; slow down time like slow motion in visual story), and how long it takes for an audience to experience the shared story.

As a storyteller, one must make choices about representing the time of the sequence of events within a story. When sharing that story with an audience, a storyteller must consider not only how long the telling of the story will take, but also how the audience will experience that time as well. While we consider the ways in which audiences experience the storytelling event itself, we see these as mostly being decisions that are made with the constraints and options available for the particular kind of story being told. For example, Ira Glass and the other storytellers for the radio show *This American Life* use music and silence breaks within and between stories to create a particular experience for their audiences; however, their choices also have a limited range due to their show being on the radio.

Some stories cover mere seconds or minutes (e.g., "An Occurrence at Owl Creek Bridge"), and other stories cover generations (e.g., *The Godfather*, *Legends of the Fall*). One of the decisions a storyteller must make is one of putting boundaries around time within the story itself. Related questions of the time frame include:

- Which events are worth recounting, dramatizing, and sharing in a story? When do those events begin and end?
- What is the order of events that a character experiences and is that the best order for my audience to experience that character's story?
- When do I want to slow down time and when do I want to speed it up?

The Common Core State Standards describes the goal of narrative writing in its third anchor standard that reads, "Write narratives to develop real or imagined experiences or events using effective technique, well-chosen details, and well-structured event sequences." It places "events" and "event sequences" front and center of what it considers important for writing narratives. Doing so means that a writer must decide where to put the boundaries around time so that it becomes an "event" or an "event sequence."

In other words, what counts as an "event"? Some narrative theorists define "event" as "a change of state, creating a more or less salient and lasting alteration in the storyworld. Events can be subdivided into temporally extended processes, deliberately initiated actions, and happenings not brought about intentionally by any agent" (Herman, McHale, and Phelan 2010, 300). As these theorists define event, time can be shaped into an event when something alters the storyworld in a notable way. This seems to be a fairly broad definition, though it does suggest criteria for storytellers when deciding how to shape time—what seems notable and what seems to have some reverberations for the world of the story and the characters in it. These criteria seem helpful in answering the question about which events are worth recounting, dramatizing, and sharing in a story; however, the definition and these criteria do not really help in deciding when an event begins and ends.

As we consider when an event begins and ends, it may be useful to consider the different types of events mentioned in the previous definition of what counts as an event. Herman, McHale, and Phelan (2010) describe three kinds of events:

1. processes that extend over time
2. actions initiated deliberately, and
3. happenings not brought about intentionally by any agent.

We imagine these kinds of events in all types of academic disciplines and in all types of careers, such as scientist, historian, mathematician, artist, and many more. Surely, each career and profession deals with processes and with deliberate and unintentional actions. These different kinds of events help us see where an event might begin and end, such as at the beginning and/or end of a process or action. Plotting things in a chronological way, perhaps with a timeline, can help a storyteller see how the characters experienced the happenings in a story and where there might be a break from what the character expected to a realization that expectation was not going to be met and a new reality awaits.

Once a storyteller has a grasp on the chronological order of events as the character has experienced it, then the storyteller must decide if that is the best way for the audience to experience the story. It is here where storytellers might decide, for example, to begin a story in media res (in the middle of things) or whether or not to use flashbacks. Schaafsma, Vinz, and National Conference on Research in Language and Literacy (2011) describe this well when they write of the choices that a narrative researcher in the classroom must make in terms of representing time:

> Chronological order is not always the best way to organize because it might not highlight aspects of the narrative that require a reader's attention. Are flashbacks useful along the way, and how are decisions made about where and why to include them? Are there intersecting tales that should be stitched together in some fashion? Maybe beginning in media res at the point of crisis or joy serves to make a particular point, that is, what anthropologists might call an emblematic tale. Knowing the repertoire

of narrative resources to manipulate and control the temporal
aspects of narrative gives the researcher choices to make, and
those choices can be determined only by the particular ways in
which individual research studies unfold. (100)

More simply, a storyteller has to decide how much time the story needs and how
that time is organized. The organization of time helps the audience experience not
only the story but the meaningfulness and point of the story. It may be chronological, but it may be something else, like using flashbacks or beginning in media res.

In addition to deciding what events are worth recounting and what order to
share those events, the storyteller must also decide how much emphasis to place
on different moments within a story. In other words, the storyteller must decide
when to speed time up and when to slow time down for the audience. Barry Lane
(1993) tackles this well and in a student-friendly way when he teaches students
how to "explode a moment" and "shrink a century." At its heart is the idea that
a storyteller can slow down the action in a scene so that the time a character is
experiencing something is slowed down and the audience can pay attention to
many details in the scene.

This is like a director of a movie or of a sporting event using slow motion
to help the audience take in more while the time within a story is slowed down.
Conversely, when a storyteller "shrinks a century," she can use just a few words to
represent a large chunk of time that the character has experienced. For instance, a
character, Harold, might be in the middle of waiting for a call from a prospective
employer. The "exploded moment" might be a moment within the interview, as
the storyteller has the audience pay attention to the sweat forming on Harold's
palms, to his thoughts of hoping that his tie is on straight and that lettuce isn't
stuck in his teeth, to him trying to remember the buzz words he wants to make
sure he hits during his next answer to the interviewer.

After the interview, Harold may spend an entire week waiting for the call
from the employer. Perhaps he's been to the grocery store, paid some bills, gone
to a friend's house for dinner, exercised each of those seven days, and watched
some baseball games on his TV. The storyteller, however, might shrink those moments that Harold experienced into just a few words, like, "After seven days, Harold heard the phone ring and knew it was the call he'd been waiting for."

The storyteller, as Bruner outlines, shapes time and focuses on particular events for the audience. Many decisions are embedded within these decisions, and clearly issues of time are connected to the other materials a storyteller must generate, including the character, the filter and slant, and the storyworld.

A variety of activities can help students manage time:

- Students can create a timeline of important events in their lives (or in the lives of a fictional character or the life of a historically important person). Have students choose one that they want to write about (and that they'd be OK sharing with others), and then have them create a timeline of the moments within the event they chose. Ask them to circle or put a star next to what they feel is the critical moment within that event. Then, give them some time to write about that one particular moment. In the next chapter, we'll look at ways students might include the thoughts of characters, descriptions, dialogue, action, and exposition (or narrative summary), but playing with timelines can help students think about how they might narrow or expand the length of an event.

- Students can be given a quick synopsis of an event (captions for newspaper or magazine photos work well), and then they can consider that moment in the event as the beginning or the end of a story (or maybe as a pivotal moment in a character's life). This can provide different starting points, which helps students see how a storyteller makes choices about how to frame a moment, which in turn shapes a story (or the audience's experience of a story) in different ways.

- Have students brainstorm a list of events or moments in a typical day. (You might want to do this as a whole class in order to have more options.) Ask students to choose a handful of those moments and then create a storyboard with those events in different order. Which moments create the surprise or break in a character's expectations?

And once again, when students have done this composing to practice and composing to plan, they need to talk together about what they did and how it worked so they can transfer what they learned to new writing contexts.

Creating a Context for the Telling of Stories

The last three of Bruner's principles remind us that every story exists within the context of other stories. That's why it's so important to develop unit contexts that support and reward the reading and writing of stories of different sorts. In their research on the literate lives of young men both in and out of school, Michael and Jeff (Smith and Wilhelm 2002) were astonished to find that the young men couldn't explain the purpose of virtually anything they were asked to do. Rev, for example, proclaimed that "English is about nothing! It doesn't help you DO anything!" (119).

We've argued here that narrative help you do *lots* of things. We need to create contexts that engage students in experiencing the power of narratives. We've found that the most effective way we can demonstrate the power of what we're teaching is to embed our instruction in inquiry units that focus on essential questions. Essential questions are the big and enduring questions that organize disciplinary conversations. And many of them are best addressed by reading and writing narratives. Think of the impact of doing the work we describe on character in a unit centered on the question "What makes a good friend? Or leader? Or parent?" Think of the impact of doing the work we describe on filter and slant in a unit built around the question "To what extent can we understand others across demographic differences?" Think of the impact of doing the work we describe on storyworlds in a unit built on the question "What makes me, me?" that includes this subquestion: "To what extent does my time and place make me who I am?" Think of the impact of doing the work we describe in managing time in a unit built around the question "To what extent am I responsible for my destiny?"

In closing, we want to stress that if we want our students to experience the power of writing narratives, we have to do more than give them the opportunity to write narratives. We have to help students learn how to get the stuff that makes a story worth telling, what we call "procedural knowledge of substance." We also have to help them learn how they can most effectively render that stuff, what we call "procedural knowledge." How we can help students develop it is the focus of our next chapter.

Shaping the Substance of Stories

*I don't necessarily start with the beginning of the book. I just start
with the part of the story that's most vivid in my imagination and work
forward and backward from there.*

—Beverly Cleary

In our previous chapter, we focused on understanding the "stuff" of which
stories are made—characters, filters/slants, storyworlds, and time—and on
how we might help students generate or discover that stuff. We refer to this
as helping students develop their "procedural knowledge of substance." But as
we explained in our discussion of the five kinds of knowledge, writers need to
know more. They also need to know how to shape that content effectively. In this
chapter, we explore how to help students do that shaping through action, description, dialogue, states of mind, and exposition. We refer to this as helping students
to develop "procedural knowledge of form."

Developing Procedural Knowledge of Form

Shaping Characters

➤ *CCSS connection*

The Common Core State Standards (CCSS) focus much of the standard for writing narratives on the ways in which writers can shape characters. The following
is how they describe the moves writers at different grade levels make to create
imagined or real characters.

46

Grade	Shaping Characters
K	N/A
1	N/A
2	"Include details to describe actions, thoughts, and feelings."
3	"Introduce . . . characters . . . use dialogue and descriptions of actions, thoughts, and feelings, to develop experiences and events or show the response of characters to situations."
4	"Orient the reader by . . . introducing . . . characters . . . use dialogue and descriptions of actions, thoughts, and feelings to develop experiences and events or show the response of characters to situations."
5	"Orient the reader by . . . introducing . . . characters . . . use narrative techniques, such as dialogue, description, and pacing, to develop experiences and events or show the response of characters to situations."
6	"Engage and orient the reader . . . introducing . . . characters . . . use narrative techniques, such as dialogue, pacing, and description, to develop experiences and events and/or characters."
7–8	"Engage and orient the reader by . . . introducing a narrator and/or characters . . . use narrative techniques, such as dialogue, pacing, and description, to develop experiences and events and/or characters."
9–12	"Engage and orient the reader by . . . introducing . . . characters . . . use narrative techniques, such as dialogue, pacing, description, reflection, and multiple plot lines, to develop experiences and events and/or characters . . . use precise words and phrases, telling details, and sensory language to convey a vivid picture of . . . characters."

When we consider the options writers have in shaping characters, we note that entire books have been written on the subject. In fact, put in the search term "creating characters" at Amazon.com, and you'll see one hundred results. For instance, you'll find the following books:

- *Creating Characters with Personality: For Film, TV, Animation, Video Games, and Graphic Novels* by Tom Bancroft (2006)
- *Creating Characters: A Writer's Reference to the Personality Traits That Bring Fictional People to Life* by Howard Lauther (1998)
- *Creating Character Emotions* by Ann Hood (1998)
- *Creating Characters: How to Build Story People* by Dwight V. Swain (1990)
- *Truth: Personas, Needs, and Flaws in the Art of Building Actors and Creating Characters* by Susan Batson (2007).

And many, many more. You might also check out Michael and Jeff's *Fresh Takes on Teaching the Literary Elements* (2010), which devotes a quarter of their book to reading, interpreting, and composing character.

Just a glimpse at this list shows the range of resources available to writers and teachers of writers: It can feel overwhelming. At the same time, we hope that it also seems productive and hopeful to have such a wide range of resources to find ideas to help students practice in shaping characters. Despite the many resources that focus on the ways in which authors can shape characters, we focus on a few major decisions, or crux moves, we see as key for our students, particularly in terms of action, description, state of mind, exposition, and dialogue.

Writers ask the following questions to themselves about the characters they are shaping:

- Description: What does the character look like?
- Action: What does the character do? And, what does the character do in relation to other characters or to places?
- Dialogue: What does the character say, especially in those moments of tension with other characters?
- State of mind: What does the character think and feel about the past (flashback), about the future (flash-forward), about the options in front of her (brain argument) (Harper 1997; Lane 1993)?
- Exposition: What does the narrator explicitly say to the audience about the character?

➤ *Lesson idea*

To help students learn how to shape characters, we suggest asking them to craft dramatic scenes as a kind of composing to practice. According to Rosenfeld, dramatic scenes are "the vehicle for emotional content," and they show a character interacting with others as a precursor to a turning point (2008, 127). One of the reasons we like students to create dramatic scenes is because they often see narratives as solely about action, rather than about how those actions provide possibilities for characters to experience an inner or outer change.

To help yourself generate different prompts, you can think with the chart that follows.

Character the Writer Wants to Follow (Use WAGS)	Second Character the Original Character Needs (Use WAGS for This Character Too)	Confined Space	What the Character the Writer Wants to Follow Could Learn About Him- or Herself as a Result of This Encounter
Waiter	Customer	Restaurant booth	Assertiveness
Corporate employee	Delivery person	Elevator	Humility
Librarian	Little child	Reading corner	Empathy

In each of these kinds of activities, we have the students work with our provided prompts, but then we ask them to use the chart to generate their own scenarios, in pairs and then alone.

The idea is to provide opportunities for writers to craft scenes that dramatize how a character is beginning to change. Such a scene demands that writers choose how to shape the character by using dialogue, action, description, state of mind, and/or exposition. Such a scene also suggests scenes before and after it, and we think that is generative for you and the writers in your classroom.

We often ask students to act out the scene before they write and then to begin their drafts by writing down what they said and did as accurately as possible. We always ask them to share what they have written with each other. For example, one pair of students could share their scenes with another pair. Each reader should identify the detail that works best to communicate the trait that the writer was trying to communicate. In a whole-class discussion, students could share the details that they selected. You could categorize those details in terms of the five primary moves authors have for shaping characters (description, action, dialogue, state of mind, exposition) and work on developing anchor charts that articulate what makes an effective use of each. As we noted in Chapter 3, such meta-conversations are essential for fostering transfer. And as you work with the charts, students will develop declarative knowledge of the writer's craft.

In addition to having students create dramatic scenes (those scenes that focus on the emotions within a character right before she experiences a turning point), we'd also suggest having students engage in activities that help them use

> ➤ *Lesson idea*

description, dialogue, exposition, action, and state of mind to shape characters. We've found the following procedure to be useful in fostering that engagement:

1. Students create a collection of characters (maybe 5–10, using the WAGS test or simply a list of potential names for characters).

2. Students choose one character to work with and place the character in a confined space (could be a physical space like an elevator or an automobile or an emotional space like the feeling of longing or restlessness).

3. Within that space, students introduce a second character for the main character to interact with—someone who pushes the first character's buttons in some way (an annoying habit, an unbearable scent, a grating voice, etc.), but is prohibited from addressing the issue because the second character has some sort of power over the first (e.g., a boss, a relative, an elder, a coach, etc.).

4. Students write for 10 minutes only reporting what happens in the exchange between the two characters (exposition, action).

5. Students pair up and share.

6. Students then write for 10 minutes only using dialogue between the two characters (dialogue).

7. Students pair up and share.

8. Students then write for 15 minutes combining the first two (action and dialogue).

9. Students pair up and share.

10. Students then find two places to add what the first character is thinking (state of mind), and then find places to add details that describe the storyworld without naming the place (i.e., students can't write, "In the elevator"; instead, they might write, "The lights began to flicker on the smudged button for the seventh floor . . .").

Shaping Filters and Slants

➤ CCSS connection

The CCSS also pay significant attention to the shaping of filters and slants.

Grade	Shaping Filters and Slants
K	"Use a combination of drawing, dictating, and writing to narrate a single event or several loosely linked events, tell about the events in the order in which they occurred, and provide a reaction to what happened."
1	"Recount two or more appropriately sequenced events."
2	"Recount a well-elaborated event or short sequence of events."
3	"Introduce a narrator . . . use dialogue and description of actions, thoughts, and feelings to develop experiences and events or show the response of characters to situations."
4	"Orient the reader by . . . introducing a narrator . . . use dialogue and description of actions, thoughts, and feelings, to develop experiences and events or show the response of characters to situations."
5	"Orient the reader by . . . introducing a narrator . . . use narrative techniques, such as dialogue, description, and pacing, to develop experiences and events or show the response of characters to situations."
6–7	"Engage and orient the reader by . . . introducing a narrator . . . use narrative techniques, such as dialogue, pacing, and description, to develop experiences and events and/or characters."
8	"Engage and orient the reader by establishing . . . a point of view and introducing a narrator . . . use a variety of transition words, phrases, and clauses to convey sequence and signal shifts from one time frame or setting to another, and show the relationships among experiences and events."
9–10	"Engage and orient the reader by . . . establishing one or multiple point(s) of view, and introducing a narrator . . . use narrative techniques, such as dialogue, pacing, description, reflection, and multiple plot lines, to develop experiences, events, and/or characters . . . provide a conclusion that follows from and reflects on what is experienced, observed, or resolved over the course of the narrative."
11–12	"Engage and orient the reader by . . . establishing one or multiple point(s) of view, and introducing a narrator . . . use narrative techniques, such as dialogue, pacing, description, reflection, and multiple plot lines, to develop experiences, events, and/or characters . . . use a variety of techniques to sequence events so that they . . . build toward a particular tone and outcome (e.g., sense of mystery, suspense, growth, or resolution) . . . provide a conclusion that follows from and reflects on what is experienced, observed, or resolved over the course of the narrative."

In the early grades, K–2, students recount an event or a sequence of events, but even then, students are asked to provide a reaction to the event (kindergarten). This reaction is a foundational move in helping students understand the filter and slants offered in a narrated event. Some of the other ways in which the CCSS suggest writers can shape filters and slants include the following:

- Use dialogue and descriptions of actions, thoughts, feelings to show a character's response to a situation.
- Use pacing, reflection, multiple plot lines, and narrators to show relationships among experiences and events.
- Provide a conclusion that follows from and reflects on what is experienced, observed, or resolved over the course of the narrative.

When writers are showing responses to, reflections on, or relationships between events and how someone has experienced those events, they are making decisions about what they want the reader to notice and experience about the events and experiences being narrated. Likewise, as readers, they must know how to attend to these constructions in a story. These are sophisticated and complex moves, and students will need significant instructional assistance and lots of opportunities for composing to practice to achieve these ends.

We suggest working with students in creating suspense scenes to practice making choices about how to shape filters and slants. We suggest this kind of scene because suspense is about "a state of uncertainty that produces anxiety" (Rosenfeld 2008, 117). In this kind of scene, a character is in some sort of jeopardy, the stakes (e.g., emotional, physical, spiritual) become more complicated during the scene, and other characters or the events exert pressure on the main character to change or act in a particular way (Rosenfeld 2008, 117). In moments of uncertainty and anxiety, a character's perspective toward the events and others in the scene becomes visible—either through what the character says, how the character acts or appears, or by what the character does not say or do.

One great way to introduce this activity is to work with students to analyze how TV shows and movies make use of this concept through the positioning of

➤ *Lesson idea*

the camera. More specifically, if the camera is positioned

- above the character, then the audience is looking down on the character and the audience is positioned in a more powerful position than the character
- at the eye level of the character, then the audience is meant to relate to the character, since the character and the audience are on the same level
- below the character, then the audience is looking up at the character and the character is positioned in a powerful way.

The camera angles help us to see the director's slant. It can also reveal the filter through which we begin to understand the character's bias. For example, the camera can be focused on the character, as in the hypothetical camera angles in the bulleted list above, or at times, the camera can show the audience what the character sees. These are simple ways to introduce the ideas of filter and slant, as well as how storytellers might deploy them to have purposeful effects on an audience.

Using the chart below can also help you create different prompts to help students create suspense scenes with a focus on filters and slants. Because suspense scenes are those that create uncertainty, it helps writers if there is an unexpected relationship between the event the character is facing and the attitude one might normally expect to read about in this kind of story. For example, below we see a slant of contempt for pastor/priest/rabbi at a teen-group retreat, which is typically not what one would expect (though we are sure that someone has experienced such a feeling during that kind of moment).

➤ *Lesson idea*

Character a Writer Wants to Follow (Use WAGS)	Event the Character Is Facing	Slant Toward the Character and the Events the Character Faces	Dialogue, Status Detail Description, Exposition, Characters' Thoughts, Action That Might Reveal This Attitude
A mom-aged woman	Speaking to her friends at 6:00 a.m. in a coffee shop after their 5:00 a.m. aerobics class	Sympathy	Status details: beat-up tennis shoes vs. the fancy shoes of the character's friends
A pastor/priest/rabbi, etc.	At the closing of a teen-group retreat	Contempt	Unflattering description of the main character (e.g., a vein in his forehead when he speaks angrily); the condescending tone when he speaks to young people
A chef at a bakery	A realtor suggesting the chef sell her bakery	Pride	A set of recipes handed down from the previous owner of the bakery; the care for her cooking equipment

The idea with this kind of prompt is to have the character face some sort of uncertainty. That is, the character doesn't know how things will turn out at the end of the scene (and neither does the reader). When faced with uncertainty, people's anxiety is increased and their guard is often down, which provides opportunities for readers to learn about a character's character. The revelation of a character's character, in turn, provides an audience with a chance to judge the way they view a character—and that judgment is informed in part by the slant a narrator takes toward the character and the events facing the character. The storyteller can use dialogue, description, action, states of mind, and exposition to shape the filter and slants that shape or inform the reader's experience.

Once again, we suggest having the students work with our provided prompts and then use the chart to generate their own scenarios, in pairs and then alone. Once again, we encourage you to have students act out the scene before they write and then begin their draft by writing down what they said and did as accurately as possible. Finally, once they are done their acting and writing, it's crucial for them to share and discuss their work so they can apply what they've learned in new situations.

Students can get additional practice shaping filters and slants in an activity we adapted from Alice LaPlante (2007) that we call "Confrontation." We suggest the following steps in working with students on that activity:

1. Students create two characters in a situation in which Character A confronts Character B as having done something wrong or as having broken the role or rules in some way.

2. Write the confrontation first through Character A's filter. Show how this character distorts things in his or her favor.

3. Then write the confrontation through Character B's filter. Show how this character distorts things in his or her favor.

4. Revise one of the confrontations in a way that shows you really love or hate the character through whom you are filtering the confrontation.

➤ *Lesson idea*

A great follow-up is an activity we call "How You See It," that we've adapted from Tom Grimes (Johnston 2007, 142). We suggest the following sequence of steps:

1. Have students pick a specific place (e.g., a lunchroom, a jail cell, a tree house, a railroad car, a garden, a stadium, a junkyard, etc.).

2. Students write a description of the place through the filters of five different characters. At least one character should be someone who knows the place well. At least one character should be someone who is seeing the place for the first time. This is practice for how characters filter places (whereas the first activity is practice for how characters filter other characters).

3. Students could also write a description from their own perspective. Only this time, they describe the place as though it holds a strong, positive memory for themselves. Then they describe the place as though it holds a strong, negative memory for themselves. They cannot mention the memory in what they write. This is practice for slants.

Shaping Storyworlds

The CCSS also asks students to shape the worlds of stories through the language of establishing and setting out situations and contexts. As with Jim's example with Mr. O'Conner and his home, the CCSS makes a point to link storyworlds with characters in the terms of "showing a response of characters to situations":

➤ *CCSS connection*

Grade	Shaping Storyworlds
K–2	N/A
3	"Establish situations . . . use dialogue and descriptions of actions, thoughts, and feelings to . . . show the response of characters to situations."
4	"Orient the reader by establishing a situation . . . use dialogue and description of actions, thoughts, and feelings to . . . show the response of characters to situations."
5	"Orient the reader by establishing a situation . . . use dialogue, description, and pacing to . . . show the response of characters to situations."
6–8	"Engage and orient the reader by establishing a context . . . use a variety of transition words, phrases, and clauses to convey sequence and signal shifts from one time frame or setting to another."
9–10	"Engage and orient the reader by setting out a . . . situation . . . use precise words and phrases, telling details, and sensory language to convey a vivid picture of the . . . setting."
11–12	"Engage and orient the reader by setting out a . . . situation . . . and its significance . . . use precise words and phrases, telling details, and sensory language to convey a vivid picture of the . . . setting."

Having students work on the initial scenes of a piece provides powerful practice shaping storyworlds because writers have to make decisions about when and how to orient and engage readers with the setting. Rosenfeld (2008) describes first scenes as those introducing a significant situation and the hero's goals, while at the same time establishing a "distinct, rich setting and subtly evoke the sense without being overbearing" (105). Writers might ask themselves questions like the ones Rebecca McClanahan (1999) implies in *Word Painting: A Guide to Writing More Descriptively*:

- When do I introduce a story's setting?
- How do I organize that description?
- How do I weave that description of setting into action, dialogue, and exposition?
- What details should I include about the place, about the time, and about the characters to evoke a particular atmosphere to the storyworld?

McClanahan offers a variety of techniques writers use to enact their answers to those questions, including the following:

- The "front-loading method" in which the "setting almost acts as a character, the first character arriving onstage" (1999, 179). This is when the writer decides to introduce details of the storyworld in the very first few lines to the piece, and she suggests that readers might be more patient with this method in longer pieces (like novels) rather than in shorter stories (like short fiction or poetry).
- The "person then place method" in which the character or narrator is first introduced and then the storyworld is described through that person's filter or slant. The person might be positioned in a stationary place and then positional words or phrases (e.g., *to my right*, *over my head*, *I turned around*, etc.) point the reader to parts of the landscape. Or, the landscape might be stationary, but appear to be moving, because the person is moving.
- The "one detail method" is when one element of the setting stands out and everything is put in relation to that detail (e.g., might be an ocean or a mountain or a parking lot, etc.).
- The "other senses method" is when a writer chooses to use a sense other than sight to orient the reader to the world of the story (e.g., the sound of a freight train, the smell of a cow field, the feel of the cold wind, the taste of the cafeteria macaroni and cheese, etc.).

We think it is helpful to have students write and collect many opening scenes to many potential stories to help them learn how to shape storyworlds. This can constitute composing both to practice and to plan. First scenes can open in a number of ways, but they tend to orient the audience by establishing five threads of time, place, character, mood, and subject (Franklin 1986). We use these five threads as a way to help us create prompts for students to practice shaping and presenting storyworlds:

➤ *Lesson idea*

Character the Writer Wants to Follow (Use WAGS)	Place: Where Is the Character?	Time: When Is It for the Character?	Mood: What Do You Want the Reader to Feel?	Subject: What Is on the Character's Mind?	What Orienting Method Do You Want to Use for Describing the Scene?
A young boy	In his backyard	The morning after he built his fort	Excitement	The promise of playing in his fort with his neighborhood friend	Person then place method
A sheltered sixteen-year-old	A subway	The first subway ride in the city	Awe	Being around a diverse group of people	Front-loading method
A basketball coach for seven-year-old girls	A pizza place	On a first date with a woman he likes	Nervousness	Wanting the date to go well, but frustrated that players on his team happen to be at the restaurant with their families	Other senses, especially the sense of smell

The idea behind this kind of prompt is to provide opportunities for students to practice creating opening scenes that help orient their potential readers to a story. Of course, the heuristic in the previous chart might also be a tool for students to use to create many possible opening scenes, and they might be surprised to discover which opening scenes they practice writing seem to have the most energy behind them. We like having our students draft multiple opening scenes, especially in informal ways, so that they can choose what they might want to pursue in more extended pieces.

And after they've written, once again it's important for them to talk. That is, after coming up with potential opening scenes and after having practice drafting a few opening scenes, students should share which opening scenes they want to pursue and why. Which openings are the most compelling for them as writers? Which openings are the ones that lead them to wonder about the story that follows?

In addition to practicing and planning first scenes, we suggest working with students to provide multiple, but connected, opportunities to present storyworlds though various filters of different characters. We've adapted an idea from Rebecca Johns (Johnston 2007, 269–71) that she calls "A Stranger Comes to Town" to do so. We suggest proceeding as follows:

1. Students draw a diagram, with as much detail as possible, of a town or street in a story.

2. Students then mark locations on the diagram where interesting or important things might happen.

3. Students write, then share, a paragraph that describes the most interesting of the events through the filter of someone who is native to the town.

4. Students then choose one house in that town or street that will be of major importance to the story, and they draw a detailed diagram of it. Again, they mark spots in the house where interesting or important events occur. Students choose one event and write a paragraph about it through the filter of someone who lives in the house.

5. Students then choose one room in the house that is of particular importance to the story. Again, they draw as detailed a diagram of the room as possible.

6. Students then describe one important event that occurred in the room through the filter of the room's occupant.

7. Students then introduce a stranger to the story by describing the town, the house, and the room through the filter of that stranger.

8. Finally, students introduce one of the native residents to the stranger, and they write a conversation between the two.

Shaping Time

Finally, when we examine the CCSS writing standard 3 at the different grade levels, we see the kind of choices storywriters have to make in shaping time. In particular, notice that authors must make decisions that include the following:

➤ *Writing standard 3, different grade levels*

- which chunk of time to share in a story
- how to organize the events within a story
- how to highlight important moments in time for audiences
- when to begin and close the presented time in a story for an audience, and
- how to link events together.

Grade	Shaping Time
K	"Tell about the events in the order in which they occurred."
1	"Recount two or more appropriately sequenced events . . . use temporal words to signal event order, and provide some sense of closure."
2	"Recount a well-elaborated event or short sequence of events . . . use temporal words to signal event order, and provide a sense of closure."
3–5	"Clear event sequences . . . organize an event sequence that unfolds naturally . . . use temporal words and phrases to signal event order . . . provide a sense of closure."
6–7	"Well-structured event sequences . . . organize an event sequence that unfolds naturally and logically . . . use a variety of transition words, phrases, and clauses to convey sequence and signal shifts from one time frame or setting to another . . . provide a conclusion that follows from the narrated experiences or events."
8	"Well-structured event sequences . . . organize an event sequence that unfolds naturally and logically . . . use a variety of transition words, phrases, and clauses to convey sequence and signal shifts from one time frame or setting to another, and show the relationships among experiences and events . . . provide a conclusion that follows from the narrated experiences or events."
9–10	"Well-structured event sequences . . . create a smooth progression of experiences or events . . . sequence events so that they build on one another to create a coherent whole . . . provide a conclusion that follows from and reflects on what is experienced, observed, or resolved over the course of the narrative."
11–12	"Well-structured event sequences . . . create a smooth progression of experiences or events . . . sequence events so that they build on one another to create a coherent whole, and build toward a particular tone and outcome (e.g., a sense of mystery, suspense, growth, or resolution, . . . Provide a conclusion that follows from and reflects on what is experienced, observed, or resolved over the course of the narrative."

We suggest that students practice the shaping of time by writing action scenes, because a story writer is able to determine which actions to show and the pace of those actions. In other words, we consider what Barry Lane (1993) considers "exploding a moment" or "shrinking a century." More specifically, writers can have their audiences see events unfolding slowly—like it would in a slow-motion replay of a sporting event, which Lane labels an "exploded moment." Or, writers can have its audiences skip over long stretches of time in just a few words, such as, "The 1908 Chicago Cubs celebrated their World Series win. One hundred and four years later, Cubs fans are still waiting to celebrate again."

When slowing down or speeding up a scene, a writer is making decisions about how much to emphasize description, dialogue, exposition, and states of mind. For instance, writers might not only signal the beginning and end of a scene with temporal words, but also by the way in which they set the scene. A writer might, for instance, begin with a "wide-angle" view of the scene's setting, then zoom in on a character's actions, and then end the scene with another "wide-angle" view of the scene's setting. The readers' experience of time is slowed down at the beginning and end of the scene, and then it is sped up during the heart of the action.

Another decision might be how to use dialogue in an action scene in order to shape time. For instance, in speeding up a scene, a writer might not use dialogue tags, as well as have characters speak in short sentences. Or, the writer might use a piece of dialogue to break up a stretch of action. Think here not of fiction stories, but maybe of a story you might see on the news or on a sports highlight show. The announcer sets the scene, providing some orienting and contextual details, shows some of the action from the event, and then has a character or two provide commentary with a few bits of dialogue. The idea is that the action from the clips is contained and that there is some contextual setup to begin and some commentary from participants to close. The process involves knowledge of context and purpose, of substance, and of form; it also involves planning, practicing, composing, and reflecting—thereby covering the various kinds of knowledge and composing.

When working with action scenes, students have to make decisions about all that the CCSS lay out in regards to shaping time.

- On the beginning and ending of the chunk of time shared: When and how do I begin and end the action?

- On organizing events: How do I show and organize the steps a character takes in moving forward toward her goal? How do I link events logically and clearly?

- On highlighting important moments: How do I build the events to reveal the consequences and changes the character will face because of these actions?

The CCSS suggest some of the ways in which story writers can shape time, particularly by how one presents action. These ways include the following:

- Use temporal words and phrases to signal the order of events.

- Use a variety of transition words, phrases, and clauses to convey sequence.

- Use a variety of transition words, phrases, and clauses to signal shifts from one time frame to another.

- Sequence events for particular effects, including the effect of a coherent whole to the story and the effect of building a particular tone and outcome.

- Provide closure or a closing that signals the end of the story, that follows the logic of the events preceding it, and that reflects on what is experienced, observed, or resolved over the course of the narrative.

The following chart has been useful for us as we work with students to help them shape time.

➤ *Lesson idea*

Character a Writer Wants to Follow (Use WAGS)	What Is the Character Doing to Pursue His or Her Goal?	What Are the Internal and External Obstacles That Make This Pursuit of the Goals Difficult?	What Moment Is It Really Important for the Audience to Pay Attention?
An elderly woman in the neighborhood	Walking the neighborhood	Internal obstacle: losing her memory External obstacle: getting colder outside	The moment when she is almost knocked down by a young person riding her bike with friends

(continues)

Character a Writer Wants to Follow (Use WAGS)	What Is the Character Doing to Pursue His or Her Goal?	What Are the Internal and External Obstacles That Make This Pursuit of the Goals Difficult?	What Moment Is It Really Important for the Audience to Pay Attention?
An eighth-grade boy at a school dance	Asking girls to slow dance with him	Internal obstacle: overly confident and not reading (or perhaps he's ignoring?) cues External obstacle: guys on his basketball team are giving him a hard time and the dance is wrapping up	The moment when he approaches the girl (who he doesn't know likes him) right before the dance ends
A young girl	Just leaving her home and heading down the block	Internal obstacle: doesn't really want to go, but feels committed External obstacle: neighborhood seems so big and dangerous, especially the big and loud dogs on her block	The first time she confronts the dog

Notice that these prompts focus on how writers shape the boundaries of time (e.g., when the scene begins and ends), as well as how to speed up or slow down the reader's and character's experience with time. For example, the final column, "What Moment Is It Really Important for the Audience to Pay Attention?" suggests that the writer might slow down time (Lane's "explode a moment"). When storytellers ask, "What happens next?" they are asking a question about plot, which is largely the focus of time in this section. However, when storytellers ask, "How should I present and order those events for my audience?" they are asking a question about structure. In the final section of this chapter, we look at how story tellers use a complication–resolution framework in order to structure narratives.

Another possibility is an activity we call "Time to Travel." It proceeds as follows:

- Students list various vehicles for travel—a train, a bus, a car, a plane, a bike, a skateboard, a helicopter, and so on, and then choose one.
- Students write a description of what it is like for one person to head on a trip though the chosen means of travel.
- Students write a paragraph or brief scene in which the character is stuck, can't move quickly, but needs to get somewhere. Include what the character is thinking, what the character says to him- or herself or to others, what the character sees and hears. Not much actual time is ticking, but it seems to the character like it is taking forever. The

character might be stuck with a person she or he doesn't want to be with at the moment, but can't reveal that disinterest.

- Next, students write a paragraph or brief scene in which the character is in that mode of travel with someone she or he really wants to reveal an interest in, but can't muster up the words quickly enough. Not much time is passing, but it feels as though it's ticking so very quickly.

- In each paragraph or brief scene, include set pieces (objects tied to the space, like a steering wheel or a door) and surrounding elements (like weather or other people the characters don't meet).

Remember that in each of these kinds of activities, we have the students work with our provided prompts, but then we ask them to use the chart to generate their own scenarios, in pairs and then alone, and to discuss them in both small and large groups.

As students do the work we've described to help them shape characters, storyworlds, and time, they can be assisted by reading and talking about mentor texts. Figure 4.1 provides some suggestion of mentor texts compiled by the Middleton Thinking Partner Team.

Figure 4.1   Possible Mentor Texts Compiled by the Middleton Thinking Partner Team (Kim Brocke, Jayna Eichelberger, Cheryl Forse, Robin Renee Gilbert, Jelena Maxwell, Nicole Mitchell, Gretchen Smith, and Angela Young)

	FICTIONAL	NONFICTION
Characters • Who change (or face the possibility of change), especially in values • Who experience something other than what they expected	*Poppy*, Avi *Flawed Dogs*, Berkley Breathed *Chicken Sunday*, Patricia Polacco *The Miraculous Journey of Edward Tulane*, Kate DiCamillo *Rifles for Watie*, Harold Keith *Love That Dog*, Sharon Creech *Matched*, Ally Condie *The Book Thief*, Markus Zusak *Because of Winn-Dixie*, Kate DiCamillo *The Invention of Hugo Cabret* and *Wonderstruck*, Brian Selznick *Thundercake*, Patricia Polacco *Mailing May*, Michael O. Tunnell	*The Trouble Begins at 8: A Life of Mark Twain in the Wild, Wild West*, Sid Fleischman *Lincoln: A Photobiography*, Russell Freedman

(continues)

Figure 4.1   *Continued*

	FICTIONAL	NONFICTION
Storyworlds • That have their own rules that characters must adhere to and that create constraints for characters to grapple with	*Hunger Games*, Suzanne Collins *The Line Away*, Teri Hall *Inkheart*, Cornelia Funke *Dinotopia*, James Gurney *The Giver*, Lois Lowry *The Pretties* and *The Uglies*, Scott Westerfeld *City of Ember*, Jeanne DuPrau *Fablehaven*, Brandon Mull	*We Are the Ship*, Kadir Nelson *Through My Eyes: Ruby Bridges*, Ruby Bridges *The Children of Topaz*, George W. Chilcoat and Michael O. Tunnell *One Thousand Tracings: Healing the Wounds of World War II*, Lita Judge
Time • Puts boundaries on a specific events (think one scene) or on a specific series of events (think a chain of scenes)	*Esperanza Rising*, Pamela Muñoz Ryan *The Greatest Skating Race: A World War II Story from the Netherlands*, Louise Borden and Niki Daly *The Little Ships: The Heroic Rescue at Dunkirk in World War II*, Louise Borden	*The Dreamer*, Pamela Muñoz Ryan and Peter Sis *Amelia and Eleanor Go for a Ride*, Pamela Muñoz Ryan *Marian Sang: The True Recital of Marian Anderson*, Pamela Muñoz Ryan *Henry's Freedom Box: A True Story from the Underground Railroad*, Ellen Levin and Kadir Nelson *Lafayette and the American Revolution*, Russell Freedman's Library of American History, Russell Freedman
Filter and slant (Think about this in terms of the *Wonder Years*. The filter is who the audience follows, namely Kevin as a kid. The slant is the nostalgic look back from Kevin as an adult.) • Open to interpretation • Leads to more questions, rather than answers	*Thank You, Mr. Falker*, Patricia Polacco *Poppy*, Avi *Hatchet*, Gary Paulsen *Junkyard Wonders*, Patricia Polacco	*Tracking Trash: Flotsam, Jetsam, and the Science of Ocean Motion* (Scientists in the Field series), Loree Griffin Burns (sections in narrative) *Left for Dead: A Young Man's Search for Justice for the USS Indianapolis*, Pete Nelson, Hunter Scott *How Pictures Work*, Molly Bang *The Mary Celeste: An Unsolved Mystery from History*, Jane Yolen *The Children of Topaz: The Story of a Japanese-American Internment Camp: Based on a Classroom Diary*, George W. Chilcoat and Michael O. Tunnell

Shaping Scenes into Stories

Thus far we've suggested working with scenes as a way for students to do the composing to practice to develop procedural knowledge of form. But, of course, most stories have more than one scene, so storytellers also have to be able to arrange scenes to achieve their intended effects.

Narratives often follow a complication–resolution framework, at both the scene and whole-text levels (Franklin 1986). When writers are working at the scene level, the character we follow is faced with a complication that is resolved or heightened by the end of the scene. When writers are working at the whole-text level, characters are faced with a complication that is resolved at the end of the piece; that is, the tension of pursuing an important goal has been relieved and the character has changed in some way as a result.

Of course, some of the complications and resolutions vary depending on the recognizable structure. More specifically, we refer here to the kinds of stories that Joseph Campbell outlines in *The Hero with a Thousand Faces* (2008). Writers can shape scenes and stories that work together in a predictable, recognizable, mythic structure. Nick Morgan, a political and business speechwriter and rhetorician, refers to some of these kinds of structures as a "Quest," a "Stranger in a Strange Land," a "Romeo and Juliet," and "Revenge" (Morgan 2003). Each of these kinds of stories suggests particular ways of structuring and sequencing events.

For example, in a quest, the complication is that the character we follow heads out to pursue some important goal—a goal significant both personally and to a larger community. As the character is on the journey, she or he faces obstacles, meets mentors, faces enemies, and can return home feeling different—usually transformed and more valuable to the community. Campbell describes this general pattern as the hero quest archetype. This kind of story is structured in a linear, chronological way (e.g., *Lord of the Rings*).

On the other hand, a stranger in a strange land structure finds a character in new surroundings. The disorientation makes the character question him- or herself, and as the character engages with the new situation, she or he begins to realize that things are not all that different (e.g., pick a story with a new teacher, like say *Dangerous Minds* or even *Welcome Back, Kotter*). The point here is that stories are structured with a complication–resolution framework, and it is up to the writer how to present those parts to the audience.

This complication–resolution framework illustrates a cause/effect way of thinking. For example, "Character A does X, which means that Y happens. Because Y happens, then Character X does Z." This is what Madison Smartt Bell (1997) refers to as a "linear story structure," and it is the kind of structure often represented by the Freytag Pyramid you might find in textbooks or in handouts. The pyramid (or triangle) represents the relationship between what happens (plot) with when it happens (time). That is, Event A happens and the complications slowly build until there is a climax that is then followed by a resolution. Many stories are structured this way. But not all are. Moreover, we think the Freytag Pyramid might be helpful as a revision tool or as a way to help figure out where a story might be out of rhythm or logic. However, we think it's problematic to use it as a planning tool. When students use the Freytag Pyramid as a way to plan a story, we find their stories are less about the character and much more about trying to make information fit into the "right" place in the "right" way.

Moreover, this kind of story structuring is not the *only* way to structure a story. Writers might also use what Bell refers to as a "modular design structure." Bell (1997) writes about the linear design and the modular design in this way:

> If linear design can be understood as somehow subtractive, a process of removing the less essential material so as to reveal the movement of narrative vectors more cleanly and clearly, the modular design is additive. The writer adds and arranges more and more modular units which may be attractive in themselves for all sorts of different reasons, but which also must serve the purpose of clarifying the overall design of the text as a whole . . . What modular design can do is liberate the writer from linear logic, those chains of cause and effect, strings of dominoes always falling forward. Modular design replaces the domino theory of narrative with other principles which have less to do with motion (the story as a process) and more to do with overall shapeliness (the story as a fixed geometric form) . . . Time is always a tyrant over all narratives: some events must always precede and others always follow. Modular design allows the writer to throw off the burden of chronology as much as is possible . . . Modular design is an attractive way to show relationships between events or people or motifs or themes which are not generated by sequences of cause and effect and are somehow atemporal, perhaps even timeless. (213–16)

Although Bell mentions a number of texts that employ a modular design (e.g., *Winesburg, Ohio* by Sherwood Anderson; *As I Lay Dying* by William Faulkner; *Love Medicine* by Louise Erdrich; *Trailerpark* by Russell Banks; *Stones for Ibarra* by Harriet Doerr; *The Beans of Egypt* by Carolyn Chute; among others), we will focus on linear design (the complication–resolution framework) because that is the kind of structure to stories we see students finding most helpful; however, we also think it can help students to play with modular designs.

Jon Franklin, a Pulitzer Prize–winning journalist, writes about the complication–resolution framework for both simple stories and for sagas (Franklin 1986). The difference is that a saga (e.g., *The Godfather*) has multiple characters and subplots, whereas the simple story follows one character and one clear plot. For Franklin, both kinds follow a complication–resolution skeleton, and when planning the structure of a piece, a writer can outline the development of a story from the complication to the resolution using three-word statements. Franklin offers the following example:

> *Complication:* Company fires Joe.
>
> *Development:*
>
> 1. Depression paralyzes Joe.
> 2. Joe regains confidence.
> 3. Joe sues company.
>
> *Resolution:* Joe regains job. (Franklin 1986, 121)

Franklin points out how each of these statements uses an active verb that involves a character the writer wants to follow (because the character must act) and that each statement represents the end of the scene that can be dramatized because each scene builds to the action in the statement. We use Franklin's kind of statements in the chart below:

➤ *Lesson idea*

Character the Writer Wants to Follow (Use WAGS)	The Complication	The Plot Development (the Order of What Happens; Use a Timeline)	The Resolution
A nurse	Patient berates Jackie.	Jackie vents to colleagues. Jackie listens to patient's son. Jackie feeds patient.	Jackie saves patient.
Punk singer	Boyfriend dumps Tilly.	Tilly drives van for tour. Tilly meets young fan. Tilly plays show.	Tilly writes letter.

Again, students can use the chart to create scenes that they dramatize, or to flesh out the outline in writing. But this kind of structured assistance should be followed by students practicing how to generate their own complication–resolution scenarios, in small groups and then individually. It should also be followed by lots and lots of talk in which students explore together what worked and what didn't, what they want to take forward, and what they want to leave behind.

➤ *Lesson idea*

Another valuable tool to use as a writer or as a teacher of writers is the newspaper. Newspapers are filled with both complications and with resolutions, and they leave the reader wondering how and why these complications arose or were resolved. That is, you and your students might use classifieds, news stories, photos and captions, obituaries, and so on as stimuli to infer the beginnings (pretexts) of stories and to access or generate the ending of stories. The creative work is imagining what happened to cause the complication and how a character or person got to this present moment and place, so work backward to consider what complication the person faced and why the person viewed it as a complication to a goal they wanted to reach.

Finally, as we think about the ways in which writers help orient their readers, we want to highlight that it is vital for our students to consider what information is known to their reader and what information is new. It is important to help students orient their readers, especially during the beginning of scenes when they have to ask themselves, "Which of the threads of this new scene is different than the threads at the end of the last scene?" The threads—character, time, subject, mood, and place—can be broken and reestablished quickly through any of the five modes of action, description, exposition, dialogue, or characters' states of mind.

In this chapter and the one that precedes it, we've explored lesson ideas that engage students in composing to practice and composing to plan as a way to help them develop the procedural knowledge of substance and form that they'll need to be able to compose compelling narratives. Being able to do so will serve them well in their lives. And they'll result in students meeting or exceeding the CCSS.

But as we argued in the close of our preceding chapter, such work can't happen in a vacuum. In our next chapters, we spin out more specifically how we can embed the instruction we're calling for into meaningful contexts.

Narrative Nonfiction

Writing About the Self

Narrative is a kind of back door into
something very deep inside us.

—Ira Glass

One quality that all human beings share, a quality that is particularly true of kids, is that we are *intensely* self-interested. As a result, we tell stories about our lives—both to ourselves and to others. These stories work to help us gain self-understanding. And they work to influence the way that others understand us.

Throughout the three-book series we've worked on together, we've shared lots of personal stories. Those stories have helped us understand ourselves as teachers, as researchers, as husbands and fathers, as friends, and as athletes or sports fans. We hope that they've worked to influence you to see us as informed and ethical practitioners who care deeply about both students and teachers.

Outside our writing, we tell many personal stories as well. We tell them in our classes to introduce ourselves and to share our experiences with an instructional strategy on which we're working. We tell them in our daily lives when we meet someone new. We tell them to make a point to our kids. We tell them on job interviews.

We often ask students to share their stories as well. A "What makes you say so?" probe about a student's prediction about what will happen next in the class' reading invites a story. So too do many college entrance essay prompts. So too do the chestnuts "Write about your most embarrassing/frightening/life-changing experience" that are the first writing assignments in many classes we've observed.

The logic behind this kind of early assignment is that we teachers want a chance to see how well students write, and we want our students to write from their own experiences and interests. This kind of writing also offers the opportunity for students to identify themselves to each other and to learn about each other early in the school year or semester.

Students are practiced at responding to these kinds of assignments. Bereiter and Scardamalia (1987) note that young writers begin writing very quickly after being given an assignment and compose at an astonishingly quick rate. They are able to do so because they are engaged in what Bereiter and Scardamalia call "knowledge telling," simply rattling off a recollection. But if we accept Ballenger's claim that "the writer's motive isn't merely to write what happened but to reflect on what he or she makes of what happened" (2011, 76), if we want our students to engage in "knowledge transforming" (in Bereiter and Scardamalia's terms), we have to help them craft compelling scenes and effectively shift between narrating the story of the past events and narrating the meaning they see in those events. The purpose of the sequence of activities we will be sharing is to help them do just that.

Composing to Plan and Developing Knowledge of Purpose and Context

As with any sequence of instruction that supports students' composing and understanding, it is important to provide a significant purpose and a meaningful context for learning and for use of what is learned. We've maintained throughout all three of our books in this set that an inquiry unit and its essential questions help to provide students not only with a clear purpose and reason to write, but also with focus, material, and potential audiences for the text they compose.

The assignment sequence we'll share here was developed by Boise State Writing Project (BSWP) fellow Greg Wilson, a middle school teacher in Idaho. The essential question that framed this unit on the topic of identity was "What makes me, me?"

Greg had this to say about the genesis of the unit and its purpose: "I teach in a middle school with a very diverse student body, both socioeconomically and ethnically. We noticed that the students didn't seem to know a lot about each other or each others' lives, and didn't even interact very much. The team decided to support a unit on 'What makes me, me?' during the second trimester of the year. The timing was based on our belief that we wanted the kids to have achieved a certain level of trust and familiarity with each other, but we wanted to leverage the gains from the unit for the rest of the year in terms of mutual respect and collaboration."

Here's the composition assignment the students received in the context of the identity unit:

> We all have personal stories to tell, and some of those stories reflect minor, or occasionally, major life-changing experiences. Your story is to be autobiographical and about one experience or situation that has shaped and affected you in some way. Perhaps you had an adventure or experience while traveling that caused you to look at the world in a different way. Maybe you discovered an activity or sport that has enriched your life. As individuals and as members of groups, we face many challenges that affect and even change us. Perhaps this kind of challenge will be at the heart of your story.
>
> Your task is to compose an autobiography of a discrete influential experience. You will then complete a multimedia PowerPoint presentation using visuals that will go along with your story.
>
> So, your goal is to write an account of an important event, activity, or situation in your life and provide images to go with it that will enrich our understanding. The pictures could be photos of places, family, friends, animals, works of art, objects, maps, or other things that help you tell your story. Once completed, you will share your PowerPoint presentation with the Red Team students and teachers. We will take two afternoons to share and enjoy each others' presentations. Our team, including teachers and staff, will be the audience.

Class time will be provided to plan, practice, draft, and finalize your composing.

Again, your goal is to write a powerful piece and support your writing with strong images that help your audience understand your story.

To get his students thinking about the possible purposes such writing could achieve, Greg and his class read some short autobiographies of discrete experience (excerpts from Maxine Hong Kingston, Booker T. Washington, Helen Keller, Ghandi, Black Elk, Malcolm X, Edward Abbey, Maya Angelou, Barack Obama, and Eminem) and brainstormed the purposes of such pieces and in what contexts they would be meaningful. The students cited the following purposes:

- to share one's experiences and thinking
- to be known and to be understood
- to convey oneself or one's sense of self
- to preserve a memory
- to preserve a legacy
- to build empathy and understanding
- to help others walk in someone else's shoes
- to understand social, cultural, and political issues and how these affect people
- to question the status quo; work for change.

As they read the autobiographical excerpts, the students engaged in several activities, both as applied to their reading and then to their own lives. The activities were designed to help students reflect upon their lives and what events and situations and forces had shaped them, with an eye to selecting a topic for their autobiography of discrete experience. As such, the activities helped students develop procedural knowledge of substance that could be use for their current piece and for extended theme autobiographies and memoirs in the future. Here is a series of steps to an activity that can easily be adapted, but that helps students tap into their own lives and practice combining experience, action, and reflection:

1. Students freewrite for 5–15 minutes about their repeated life stories. Have them begin with their birth and end with the present day. Before they begin writing, you might also have them put "I was born" on the top of the page and "And I sit in class writing my life story" on the bottom of the page. The purpose of this step is to provide students with a chance to write about themselves and to identify one moment they want to learn more about.

2. After freewriting, students read what they wrote and circle one incident they want to learn more about.

3. Once one moment is chosen, then students write some more (10 minutes or so) about the memory of that moment. Who was there? What were they doing? Where were they? What do they remember seeing, smelling, hearing, feeling? What did they want at that moment? What sticks out about this moment?

After writing about the memory of that moment, then students can write about what they think that moment means. Roy Peter Clark (2007) refers to this as helping students move up the "ladder of abstraction." At the bottom of the ladder is a scene that has been dramatized: It includes concrete details, like the details of the memory the students have just written. As students move up the ladder, they are becoming more abstract or generalized. For example, a memory Jim might write about might look like the following on the ladder of abstraction:

Top of the Ladder (Abstract and General)	Nonviolence Works—Eventually
Step on the ladder	Changing others' behavior through force is unethical and doesn't really last long-term
Step on the ladder	Hurting another person make me feel bad
Bottom of the ladder (concrete and specific)	Fight with neighbor when I was ten

Once students have written about a memory and about what they think it means, ask them to weave the two together. The idea here is to provide students with a chance to (1) write about themselves and (2) practice weaving together action and commentary.

➤ Lesson idea

Another great activity that involves students in composing to plan is making a list of "Top Ten Me-Shaping Events." Students are well aware of various top-ten lists and their functions. But to get the students to mine and reflect on their own life experiences to assist in planning for their own autobiography, Greg shared a David Letterman list and some of The Ten series books (Wilhelm). He then asked students to create a top-ten list of "me-shaping" events for one of the historical figures they had read about, and then to do one for themselves, which they did with great zeal.

➤ Lesson idea

As a follow-up, Greg had students compose a bucket list of completed, or checked-off, experiences that they thought would be cherished, valued, or important to them in some way by a historical figure throughout their lives. He then has students create a list of experiences that they think the historical figure might have enjoyed or engaged with in their lives. Then the students do the same for themselves. The students discuss how some events can shape and stay with a person and how goals and desires also express identity and shape a life.

➤ Lesson idea

The penultimate composing to plan activity involved creating an autobiographical timeline on rolls of newsprint. The timeline was to record all of the major events from the student's life that were important and shaped them in some way. Some students created the timeline like a stock chart, with up and down periods. At the conclusion of this activity, Greg had students consider what event would be the most likely one to write about in terms of how it shaped their identity and world view.

➤ Lesson idea

Because he wanted students to think about the small moments of their lives as well as the big ones, Greg followed up by adapting an activity from Kelly Gallagher's excellent book *Write Like This* (2011) based on Amy Rosenthal's book *Encyclopedia of an Ordinary Life* (2005). Rosenthal records her life as an "alphabetical existence" (35) and shares such quotidian details as what she thinks about when she buys something from a vending machine. After reading excerpts from her book, Greg asks his students to collaboratively compose a list of possibilities for *Encyclopedia of Ordinary Life* entries for a historical figure they have read about. Then individually students do a few for themselves. This helps students to see what ordinary details from their lives can also reveal something important about their identities.

Composing to Practice and Developing Procedural Knowledge of Form and Substance

To engage his students in composing to practice, Greg employed the activities we discussed in the previous chapter on shaping characters, filters and stances, storyworlds, and time. Taken together, these activities for composing to practice largely help students learn how to create or collect details, information, characters, and scenes to include in their autobiography of discrete experience. These opportunities also provide multiple chances for student to take risks as writers and to practice in a low-risk environment.

Each of these activities provides students with many chances to share with one another what they are doing as writers and why they are doing so. In other words, we do not wait for students to complete rough drafts before they are able to offer one another feedback or before they are able to serve as models for one another; instead, this sort of peer review and response is embedded throughout the sequence.

Early Draft Composing

By now, most of the work has been done. The students are like athletes who have planned and practiced for the championship event. They are ready to move into the arena. They have developed the substance of their performance and have practiced all the crux moves. Now it's time to put it all together.

Greg provided both class time and homework time for students to draft out their stories and accompanying PowerPoint presentations. He reminded the students that they needed to meet one or more of the purposes that they had articulated for autobiographies of discrete experience.

The students also solidified the criteria they had been articulating throughout the unit and tweaked them to fit the multimodal nature of their project. Their list ultimately looked like the following:

- Content: One event or situation is described. Subject matter is compelling; themes are significant and communicate a meaning that resonates with the writer's audience.

- Details: The story has a clear sense of time and place; selective details show instead of tell; we get to know the things/events/people described and they feel individual and tangible.

- Impact: The reader engages deeply in the experience of hearing and seeing this story and gains something emotional, visceral, psychological from the telling; the story lingers in the reader/listener's mind and stays with her.

- Clarity: There is a clear sense of beginning and end; the story of the event is easy to read. The reader is not left confused about anything; if things are left ambiguous, then it must be intentionally done on the part of the author.

- Originality: The story is fresh and creative and deeply personal; narrative structure, style, and subject matter combine to present the event in a provocative light that helps the audience understand the author and life in a new way.

Final Draft Composing

During the drafting, peer editors and Greg conferred to identify one personal area for focal improvement and correction on each final paper. They also identified a general problem for focal correction, and that was correcting fragment sentences. As we argue in *Getting It Right* (Smith and Wilhelm 2007), we've found that the editing process was most successful when students received two kinds of assistance: (1) general support in how to proofread and (2) explicit support in using proofreading cues for a specific focal correction area.

Greg used ideas from *Getting It Right* to provide both kinds of support. For specific support in reading for fragments, he helped the class create two sets of words: "promise words" and "beware words." *Promise words* are those that promise sentences will have two parts: relative pronouns like *which*, *who*, and so on, and subordinating conjunctions like *after*, *although*, and so on. *Beware words* are those that cause problems for more than one class member. Participles topped the list. The students kept the lists in their notebooks and then used them while employing the following tips.

Tips for Proofreading for Fragments

- Reread your paper backward, sentence by sentence.

- Read your paper aloud to other students with a double pause after each period or end stop.

- Look for –*ing* (beware) words used as verbs, and make sure they are attached to a helping verb like *is* or *was*. If not, add the helping word or change the verb.

- Look for words that promise a sentence will have two parts (e.g., relative pronouns such as *which* and *who* and subordinating conjunctions such as *after* and *although*) and make sure there are two parts of the sentence.

- Use terminology kids will transparently understand (e.g., "promise words" and "beware words").

- Help kids to research their own writing and ways to correct fragments; e.g., create lists of their own beware words as well as personal proofreading and editing lists. (Smith and Wilhelm 2007, 97)

Composing to Transfer

Throughout the reading and writing in the unit, students were engaged in formative assessments, both informally and formally. Informally, all of their planning and practicing to compose gave themselves and Greg immediate formative feedback about what they understood and could do and what they needed to learn next. And as Greg noted: "We really built a culture of success and identified as writers. The early activities were easy for the kids and they did well on them, but they were also building significant substance and skills at shaping their narratives."

More formally, every few days Greg had students briefly write down what goals they had met and what goals were next for them in progressing toward their final composition.

Because a lot of Greg's students are English language learners, he had them record their self-assessments and progress toward goals on sites like Fotobabble once a week. This helped the students practice their spoken fluency.

Greg also used the evolving criteria and rubric as a way to have students reflect, compose for transfer, and evaluate and name their progress. Carol Dweck (2006) has identified the importance for students to clearly see and name and celebrate for themselves the growth in their own knowledge. One way to do this is to have students examine a piece of writing from early in the unit, particularly in regards to specific criteria, and compare it with more recent work. Greg specifically asks students to name their improvement and to name how they know and how they achieved that improvement.

Reflecting on Greg's Unit

Greg has taught this unit for the past several years. When we talked to him about it, he confessed that it is his favorite unit and the one that is the most powerful. But he hastened to add that part of its power lay in the discomfort the presentations caused. "Despite the fact that we encourage students to consider writing about positive experiences, they gravitate toward telling about deeply personal and very challenging experiences. It surprised me because they are presenting these stories to the whole team. When I ask them about their choices, they tend to say: "Hey, this is my chance to be heard. This is a story that I need to tell. I need people to listen to this and know about it." In the first year of the unit, there were several stories that teachers and staff thought shouldn't be told, but we realized that it was the kids' choice, that they knew what they were doing, and that we would be silencing them and teaching them to be silenced if we didn't let them tell the story they wanted to tell."

Here are the topics from one class:

- a joke
- a practical joke gone wrong
- loss of a sibling
- Mexican immigration
- genocide
- divorce
- mental and physical abuse
- drug and alcohol abuse

- cancer—personal and family
- Alzheimer's
- loss of a parent
- loss of a grandparent
- incarcerated family member
- membership in urban gang
- bar mitzvah, confirmation
- asthma
- rest homes and grandparents
- value of friendship
- getting lost in the woods
- discovering something about myself
- the fear/concerns of moving to a new place
- father abandoning a family
- never knowing a parent
- loss of a family pet
- challenges of ski racing
- challenges of motocross
- a winning season
- loss of a childhood friend
- suicide of a childhood friend.

Greg is very pleased with the results of the unit. "There are a lot of kids from whom I get very little quality writing until this project. Lots of kids turn in their topics early and start drafting early. They really want to tell their story. And I have to say that though many of the stories are deeply moving and even troubling, the kids are very respectful of each other, and it seems to make a big difference to how they engage with each other and work with each other throughout the rest of the year. It's well worth doing and I will keep doing it. I guess what I am saying is this: The kids learn a lot about reading and writing, but more importantly they learn a lot about themselves and about each other. They display a lot of courage and maturity, too, both as authors and audience. It is a real growing experience for all of us, and a growing together experience too."

But stories about ourselves are not the only kinds of stories that foster the kind of growth and learning that Greg describes. Writing profiles of others can be equally compelling. It's to that kind of writing that we now turn.

Connecting to the Five Kinds of Knowledge

Greg's sequence of instruction not only helps his students craft an autobiographical piece, but it also helps his students develop the five different kinds of knowledge that we have described as (1) knowledge of purpose and context, (2) procedural knowledge of form, (3) procedural knowledge of substance, and (4) declarative knowledge of form, and (5) declarative knowledge of substance. As Greg has his students engage in crafting their autobiographical pieces, he asks students questions that help him see if students are developing their understanding of the different kinds of knowledge. In other words, the five kinds of knowledge help Greg focus his attention and questions as his students read, write, think, and share with one another throughout the course of the sequence. It might look like the following:

	Declarative Knowledge	Procedural Knowledge
Form	Understanding the features of a piece and how they are related to one another *Naming how the discrete experiences and the commentary about those experiences work together*	Knowing how to create the features of a piece that help a reader recognize it as a specific kind of piece *Shaping the piece into one that is recognizable as being autobiographical, which means that writers will need to know how to go about integrating a reporting of the events in the discrete experience along with the commentary that reveals the importance of that experience*
Substance	Understanding the concepts within a piece and how those concepts work together *How and what the discrete experience presented in the autobiographical piece reveals about how the writer sees him- or herself*	Knowing how to go about gaining that conceptual understanding *Creating characters, time, storyworld, filters/slant that reveal the events of a discrete experience that was important to the writer*

Underlying each of the kinds of knowledge in this chart, Greg is also interested in figuring out what students understand about where, when, and why people might write and share autobiographical pieces. Clearly, many of his students have a keen understanding of the purpose and contexts of autobiographical writing when they say that they want people to know who they are—they want to stake their identity and share a bit of themselves with one another. In doing so, they create and cultivate a sense of community within the classroom. Put another way, autobiographical writing can help to bring people together: It can help a group develop its group-ness. Of course, because Greg has students share their processes with one another throughout the sequence, students are developing *a shared repertoire* while they *engage mutually* in a *joint enterprise*—all of which are features of a community of practice (Lave and Wenger 1991). The "practice" in the case of the community in Greg's class is the practice of being a literate community of students who share writing and writing processes with one another.

Connecting to Narrative Principles

In this sequence of instruction that leads to autobiographical writing, or stories of the self, students are engaged in developing their sense of multiple narrative principles. Here is a reminder of the narrative principles, as we understand them.

Bruner's Terms	How We See the Features as Narrative Principles	The Substance of Stories
Canonicity and breach	A story highlights a break in what was supposed to be or what was expected to be.	Character
Intentional state entailment	A story shows changes in characters, especially in their values or in their intentional actions.	
Hermeneutic composability	A story is open to interpretation by not always being explicit about what it means.	Filter and slant
Normativeness	A story invites more questions than it poses solutions.	
Referentiality	A story adheres to the rules it creates for its storyworld.	Storyworld
Narrative diachronicity	A story shapes time.	Time
Particularity	A story focuses on a particular event or series of events.	

(continues)

Bruner's Terms	How We See the Features as Narrative Principles	The Substance of Stories
Genericness	A story is recognizable and understandable in form.	Purpose and context (implicit understanding between the audience and the storyteller)
Narrative accrual	A story builds on and is connected to other stories.	
Context sensitivity and negotiability	A story is shared for a reason and relies on the background knowledge of an audience.	

Greg's students work on a number of these, but particularly the principles that are connected to character and time. More specifically, students choose to write about discrete moments that matter to them, which means that they are focusing on a particular event and shaping it for the reader to follow and to understand why that moment matters. Often, these are moments when students were changed or faced with the possibility of changing, or at the very least, experiencing something that stood out—that broke with—the way they had previously expected things ought to be.

Not only does the work students did in the autobiography help them see how stories work in and of themselves, they also can help them see the kind of work stories do in the world. We want students to be able to understand what is going on when people tell stories because such exchanges are simply a part of their lives.

Betsy Rymes (2009) offers an extensive, flexible, and helpful set of analytical tools that students can use to help them develop that understanding. The first thing Rymes helps us think about is the situation in which a story is being shared. She breaks this down into two contexts. The first context is the "interactional context," which is simply the exchange between the teller and the audience. The second context is the broader "social context," which includes any entities (e.g., institutions, family, class, religion, gender, ethnicity, etc.) that might inform or shape the story or that might be shaped by the story.

Then, Rymes helps us focus on the actual exchange itself by presenting us with a simple and very useful heuristic that she describes as the "Into/Through/Beyond" framework. One way this framework is helpful is that it asks analyzers to put boundaries around when a storytelling event begins and ends. This is actually a bit trickier than it may seems, especially if a student is participating in the exchange or is quite familiar with all the history and background that is at play in the exchange.

- Into: What initiates this story? What event is this story embedded within? What social conditions or context is this story a response to?

- Through: How do word choices shape the characters we follow or meet within this story? How do listeners/readers coauthor the story during the telling? How does the shape of the story or the word choice within the story reveal beliefs or assumptions held in the larger social context?

- Beyond: What happens in the interaction between the storyteller and the audience once the story finishes? What might be some broader social consequences of this storytelling exchange?

This framework and the questions the framework prompts build on and extend what students have developed as they compose various narratives. These questions ask students to consider not only the story that is being shared, but also the story of the storytelling event and exchange. What seems to be the storyteller's goal? What obstacles might the storyteller have faced? What might an audience have to know or believe to find this story or this exchange compelling? What does this storytelling event reveal about the constraints and conditions of the storyteller's and/or the audience's world? Their worldviews and purposes? What are the effects and consequences of the story—on identity, belief, action, and so on? We think that when students begin to build on their own composing of narratives by investigating the ways narrative events work in their world, they will start to see narratives at play just about everywhere. This narrative competency empowers.

Conclusion

Stories of the self, like the kind that Greg's students compose, are through the writer's filter, which means readers can expect to read the writer's interpretation of the events and their significance. In the next chapter, we move on to narrative nonfiction that focuses on the stories of others. More precisely, we look at how we might write about events and experiences through other people's filter, and we ask our students to do so by composing profiles of the kind you might find in newspapers, magazines, or some websites.

CHAPTER 6

Narrative Nonfiction as Literary Journalism

Writing About Others and the World

In most cases the person I encounter is not a celebrity; rather the ordinary
person. "Ordinary" is a word I loathe. It has a patronizing air. I have come
across ordinary people who have done extraordinary things.

—**Studs Terkel,** *Touch and Go: A Memoir*

As we noted in the previous chapter, in both our personal and professional lives we tell lots of stories about ourselves. But we also tell lots of stories about others. Throughout our three books on the Common Core State Standards (CCSS), you'll especially see stories of teachers we admire. But we tell stories about other people as well. Jim tells stories of young people he's coached—players and teams who grew into something much more than they believed possible—as a way to understand how people learn with one another. Jeff's a real history buff, and he'll often sprinkle stories about some of the historical figures he finds most compelling into conversation to bring home a point about something happening to people today. Every day Michael and his wife Karen tell each other stories about the people with whom they work as a springboard for them to share ideas about how to be better colleagues and supervisors (and sometimes a way to blow off a little steam).

Even a quick look at the magazine rack of any drugstore will make it easy to see the prevalence of such stories: profiles of movie stars in gossip magazines, of candidates in newsmagazines, of CEOs in business magazines. Of course, stories of others not only abound in the popular press, they also abound in academic work. Just look at the title of these academic publications:

- *Telling Stories: The Use of Personal Narratives in the Social Sciences and History* (Maynes, Pierce, and Laslett 2008)
- *Medicine as Storytelling* (Borkan, Miller, and Reis 1992)
- Empathy, Legal Storytelling, and the Rule of Law: New Words, Old Wounds? (Massaro 1989)

In short, students will need to be able to tell the stories of others, both accurately and evocatively, both in and out of school, because it helps them understand how others see the world, which in turn provides an opportunity for students to extend, refine, or challenge the way they understand themselves. We need to plan instruction that invites students to discover and understand the way others make sense of their lives.

Composing to Plan

As we noted throughout our books, instruction is motivating if students understand why we ask them to do what we ask them to do and when they see that it's possible to do well—even with a little (or a lot of) assistance. That's why it's so important to embed the teaching of writing in a unit context in which students can experience the power and importance of the kind of writing on which we are focusing. Instruction in telling the stories of others is relevant to many, many inquiries. One context we've used with students is built around the essential question, "How do people meet challenges?" As a culminating project for this unit, we've asked students to create a profile of how one person from the community meets challenges, and we will publish this profile in a class magazine archived online. We also asked students to create a multimodal display about their informant for the community's local history museum and to present this multimodal display at a school learning fair. The assignment description reads as seen in Figure 6.1.

In composing the instructional sequence to prepare the students for the task at hand, we adapt the ideas from Wiggins and McTighe (2005), who suggest we think about performance tasks by considering the learning goals of the task, the role we

➤ *CCSS Intro, p. 7, writing anchor standard 6, compose in multimodalities, using technology to publish and share; vertical standards from grade 3*

➤ *CCSS multimodal composing standards, speaking and listening standards*

Figure 6.1

"Literary journalists write narratives focused on
everyday events that bring out the hidden patterns
of community life as tellingly as the spectacular
stories that make newspaper headlines."

—Norman Sims in "The Art of Literary Journalism"

A magazine, *Our Neck of the Woods*, is putting together a special edition that focuses on everyday people in our community doing their thing. That "thing" could be their work, their play, their hobbies, and so on. The editors have decided that the theme of the issue is "Everyday Motivation and Challenges," and they seek 800- to -1,200-word articles that help their audience learn about how people in our community see and pursue their interests in their daily lives. In other words, they want to help their readers answer the question, "How do people meet the challenges they face when they 'do what they do'?" Later, we'll extend this piece into an exhibit that you would include in our local history museum.

For now your task is to profile someone in our community in such an article so that your readers learn about how your profiled person makes sense of her or his world. You'll want to watch them in action, interview them, interview others who know that person, and maybe even research about others who do whatever it is that your person does (e.g., play an instrument, exercise, take up a hobby, do a certain job, and so on).

A strong article will . . .

• provide accurate information and details (not only about the person, the person's actions and words, but also about how the person perceives and responds to her or his challenges)

• be constructed mostly through scenes and recognizable as a narrative nonfiction magazine profile

• include and acknowledge your own experience, thoughts, questions, and so on

• connect the concrete experience of the profiled person to broader ideas about how people cope with challenges.

want students to take, the audience for the product students create, the purpose for the piece, and the criteria that would describe a strong or successful piece.

The learning goals that we imagine for our students can be put into different categories when we think about the larger unit of study. That is, we see the sequence of instruction for creating this profile for a magazine and exhibit for a local history museum as helping students move toward some, rather than for all, of the learning goals for the entire unit. More specifically, we imagine four kinds of learning goals for the larger unit.

In this particular unit, we want students to develop a conceptual understanding for the major concept of "challenge," as well as other concepts like learning, resolving, resilience, finding and retaining value in the face of challenges and loss, and so on.

We also want students to be able to meet the anchor standard for writing narrative texts as outlined in the CCSS. In particular, this standard reads that students will "write narratives to develop real or imagined experiences or events using effective technique, well-chosen details, and well-structured event sequences."

➤ *CCSS connection*

Although we see that students might deal with any (if not all) of the narrative principles that we explored earlier when crafting any narrative, we also recognize that when we design our instruction it will help us if we focus on one or two of these principles with our students. In a literary journalism piece, like the profile in a magazine, we think it is helpful to focus on how the story as presented helps the audience of the piece see how the subject's story connects with the audience member's experiences. This means that writers will have to generalize from the specific experiences of one person to connect to the audience's experiences with "challenges" more generally.

Although we want students to see themselves as readers and writers, we also want them to understand the specific kind of writing they are producing, namely magazine profile pieces, a specific example of literary journalism. This means they must develop procedural and declarative knowledge of form specific to profiles. It means that students will have to read magazine profile pieces to understand how the writers of those pieces created and manipulated the form of a magazine profile.

With these four categories of goals in mind, we can assess our students' growing understanding more purposefully throughout the sequence and not just after they have created a product. This means that we can adapt instruction to meet their current needs in ways that serve to help them progress toward the goal of composing a profile. As we outline the sequence of activities next, we highlight what we want to assess in each of the activities *and* how our formative assessments throughout the sequence work together to support our students' learning of how a narrative understanding can help them make sense of themselves, others, and their world.

Figure 6.2   Summary of the Goals

Type of Goal	Specific Goal in This Sequence
Conceptual understanding goal	Students will develop their conceptual understanding of the focus in this sequence of instruction, which is embedded in our overarching question. In this sequence, it is the concept of "challenges."
CCSS writing anchor standard 3	Students will "write narratives to develop real or imagined experiences or events using effective technique, well-chosen details, and well-structured event sequences."
Narrative principle goal	Students generalize from the specific experiences of one person to connect with the audience's experiences with "challenges" more generally.
Task or genre-specific goal	Students will understand the specific kind of writing they are producing. In the case of this sequence, it's a profile, which is one kind of literary journalism piece.

Composing to plan involves front-loading activities that will help solidify the purpose of the unit, activate students' prior knowledge, build on that knowledge as students share their responses, and provide a template for measuring understanding throughout the unit. In our first activity, we asked students what they felt were the most essential elements of living a good life. The brainstorming resulted in the following list:

➤ *Lesson idea*

- nice place to live
- parents or other adults who care and guide you
- friends and people who share your values and will work with you
- nutritious food to eat
- warm clothing
- freedom to act on one's beliefs
- sense of purpose in life
- access to education
- physical and psychological safety
- affordable health care
- respect
- clean water
- enough money
- reasonable sanitation.

We next asked students to imagine the challenge of losing one of these essential elements. What resources would they have to address the challenge? How could they imagine meeting the challenge? What obstacles might they foresee to meeting the challenge?

In a second activity, we asked students to rank the challenge of losing the following things, from most to least challenging: a friend, a cell phone, a computer, a romantic partner, a house, a country (through exile), a precious object (e.g., a watch from your grandfather), memory, health, a capacity (e.g., to read), a sense (e.g., vision or hearing). We then asked them to describe the challenge of losing the one they felt would be most difficult and to tell a story about how they might go about meeting that challenge in the healthiest way possible. These two activities work together to help students begin to think more about "challenges" and, when they share with one another, they can begin to understand how others identify and respond to challenges in a range of ways.

➤ *Lesson idea*

Composing to Practice

Now that students have a sense of the assignment and its purpose, it's time to practice developing and applying the skills they will need to complete the assignment. One of the primary tools of the researcher is that of taking notes, so that is where we start.

We begin by working with students to make concrete observations (note-taking) and making interpretations (note-making). Oftentimes, students make evaluative comments as though they are concrete details. In this activity, we want students to make a distinction between observations and interpretations, largely because they will include both in the profile they compose.

The steps we use for this activity can be found in *Ethnographic Eyes* (Frank and Bird 1999), which is a text Jeff and Jim use in a teacher research course with student teachers and mentor teachers working together on various projects. We use the following steps:

1. We show our students a photograph and ask them to take notes and write down everything they see happening. We like to begin with static images, so we project photographs or paintings. We first start with images of places without people. Then images with one person engaged in an activity. Then we use images with multiple people.

2. We write some of their notes on the board or overhead and divide them into either "note-taking" (NT) or "note-making" (NM), depending on whether it is a descriptive or interpretive detail.

3. We discuss the difference between the two sides. What was descriptive and what was interpretive?

4. Then, we move to dynamic images, so we look at videos together. Movie trailers and commercials can be helpful here because they are brief and sometimes scene-based.

5. Students continue practicing NT/NM skills with more pictures or videos, particularly those of people facing or meeting challenges as this provides for conceptual as well as procedural development that meets the inquiry theme.

The importance of these activities is to help students record and reflect—to place hold and analyze—two crux moves of literary journalism. This is an important distinction to make for thinking and writing as a scientist or other kinds of researchers. It is also very important in argumentation, where the writer has to know what is not under dispute (data) and what interpretation and reasoning is required to make the data serve a claim and do some kind of work.

Observing is one essential tool of the researcher. Another is questioning and interviewing. Learning how to ask questions that prompt others to share their stories and their take on things is a skill that can be difficult for even more experienced writers. Interviewing is a powerful kind of procedural knowledge of substance. If students learn to interview, then they have a lifelong research skill and a repertoire that will assist them in interpersonal relationships. Questioning and interviewing are well worth learning and practicing.

If students are to be successful interviewers, they have to be able to generate useful questions. To give our students an idea of the possibilities, we share approaches that Spradley (1979) delineated:

- A writer can record questions that people ask in their everyday lives (e.g., a writer researching a car salesman could listen to the kinds of questions people at a car dealership ask in that scene).

- A writer can ask "grand tour" questions (e.g., "Could you describe a typical day in the ER? Can you describe a typical conversation with a

nurse?" or variations of a grand tour question that focus more specifically on a particular task or time, such as, "Could you describe a typical report you have to write?").

- A writer can ask "example" questions (e.g., "Can you give me an example of when you learned something about a relationship?").

- A writer can ask "experience" questions (e.g., "Can you describe an
experience you had when you were new to a setting?").

- A writer can ask "direct language" questions, the kind of question that
asks someone to describe what a term means (e.g., "What does *marry-
ing* the ketchup mean?" to a person working at a restaurant).

- A writer can ask "hypothetical-interaction" questions, the kind of
question that asks a person to re-create an interaction with another
person (e.g., "What did you say and do when that customer com-
plained repeatedly and unreasonably about the food coming from the
restaurant's kitchen?").

With these kinds of questions in mind, we have students practice them as
they ask and record answers others offer in response. We typically start with having the whole class interview us as teachers, or in the role as someone else. We
then have students practice with one another and then practice some more. For
interviewing each other, we use the following process:

➤ *Lesson idea*

- Have each student identify a hobby or activity that they each do
(e.g., play the piano, draw, cook, dance, play a sport, read, play video
games, etc.).

- In groups of three, have one student be the asker of questions, one
student be the answerer of questions, and one student be the recorder
of the answers.

- The asker of questions asks different kinds of questions (see the previous list) about the answerer's hobby or interest. The recorder notes
responses.

- Students rotate roles within the triad.

- After each round of practice interviews, students debrief with one
another and with the whole class. We ask, "What questions seemed

to create the most helpful responses?" "What follow-up questions were helpful to ask?" "What was difficult about asking, answering, or recording answers?" "What did you learn about that person's hobby / interest?" "What do you want to know more about, and what questions might help you learn it?"

After rounds of interviewing one another, students might practice some more. Interviewing students from other classes or interviewing people at home, in the neighborhood, at school, or in outside groups could be helpful, especially if the student is able to practice some one-on-one interviewing. The debriefing questions could be the same or similar, and we would add questions about what was different about the different interviews.

Our students came up with the following tip sheet for interviewing after this practice:

- Phone or email to set up appointment and then confirm time and place.
- Let the subject know what you want to find out about—how they have met life challenges—so they can be thinking about it.
- Take a notebook or recording device—if you use a recorder, keep it on the whole time.
- Write down your questions but be willing to pursue new, interesting things that come up.
- Start with easy questions to put the subject at ease, then move to harder ones.
- Ask follow-up questions like: "Can you tell me more about that?" "How did you feel about that (or found the strength to do that, etc.)?"
- Ask one question at a time—don't ask multiple questions!
- Questions should be pointed and brief.
- Remember the interview is not a dialogue—get the subject to speak instead of talking yourself.
- Ask open-ended questions that can't be answered with one word or yes-or-no answers. Don't say: "Was it hard to live through the dust bowl in the depression?" Ask: "What was most challenging about living through the dust bowl in the depression?"

- Allow for silence and think time.
- Don't interrupt the subject when he or she is talking. If you think of a new question—write it down!
- Ask about negatives since this will help get at the challenges faced.

Before students interview and observe the person they will profile, it is important for students to visit or revisit key concepts from the unit. We want students to enter those observations and interviews with their own working framework of these concepts so that they have a stance to take into the conversations and observations. In our particular unit of study, the overarching question is "How do people meet challenges?" which means that three or four key concepts might include motivation, needs, risk, and feedback.

To help students solidify their conceptual understandings, we simply ask students to draw a visual that represents how they each see the relationship between the five major concepts (challenges, motivation, needs, risk, and feedback) of this unit. You might do this with note cards on a desk or maybe with sticky notes or maybe on pieces of paper. After students place the concepts in relationship to one another, have them share why they put them in that way. Students listen for patterns and outliers as others explain their choices. Alternatively, students might simply walk around and look (without explanations from one another) and then write or share what they notice across the different maps.

➤ *Lesson idea*

The idea here is that students are provided some time and opportunity to practice refining their thinking about the big concepts of the unit. In addition, they are asked to hear and listen to one another, which is a way to help them practice listening to the people they interview and observe.

Back to Composing to Plan

In this section of the instructional sequence, we move from our focus on helping students develop the ways of generating material for their magazine profiles (procedural knowledge of substance and composing to practice) to a focus on supporting students in planning and shaping that material.

We begin by reading and analyzing various profiles of people who have met or are meeting challenges. A favorite this past year was a profile of Jim Corbett, the famous British hunter of man-eating tigers. As we read several professional profiles about people who have faced historical challenges (the depression, fighting in D-day), health challenges, work challenges, and so on, we ask students to summarize the content of the profiles as well as name the moves and form of the profile, along with effects. After this, we ask students to find some of their own profiles of people facing challenges and do the same thing.

➤ *Lesson idea*

After all of this general preparation, students are ready to begin planning the particular profile they want to do. One way to help students get started is to create a relationship tree or web. Students begin by placing their names in the middle and then branching out to different categories of people they know: family, friends, neighbors, role models, teammates, and so on. Once students have a fairly extensive web of people they know, you might also ask them to create an additional layer to the web in which they add people who they would like to know. They can of course converse with family, friends, and mentors to identify other people who would be good to profile.

After adding names or types of people to the web of relationships, students can begin to narrow down whom they might want to profile. It helps here to have students write a quick paragraph or two about whom they want to interview and why. To help with this writing, you might offer students a three-column chart that has a column for physical details (what does the person look like), one for personality (mode of expression, energy level, etc.), and one for surroundings.

Once students have decided on whom they want to profile, then it is helpful to consider how they might go about observing that person. This leads to some of the logistical concerns students often face and need help navigating. One issue is simply having access to a person engaging in a practice or task. If they can't, then it becomes important for students to ask questions that prompt the person to offer retrospective accounts of doing what they do. In other words, the interview process must include questions that ask people being profiled to tell stories and provide details about what they do to meet challenges, and then students can follow up with questions that ask the interviewees to explain their thinking during those activities. For instance, if a student is interviewing a doctor, the student may not be able to be around while the doctor is working. If this kind of occasion occurs, then the student can ask situational questions that might be more like the "experience" questions or "task-related" questions that Spradley (1979) suggests. This is a critical move, because students need to include scenes in their profile pieces, because narrative nonfiction is scene-based and because scenes help readers enter the profiled person's world and filter.

Another approach is for students to observe the scene to provide some contextual details in the magazine article. One way to help students understand this kind of move is to have them watch the opening of movies in which the director establishes the scene, which is the kind of move that students could take in their articles. If they are unable to observe the person interacting within the space, then they can observe the space itself.

➤ *Lesson idea*

Planning interviews also takes some time and lots of attention to logistical details. To plan interviews, it is helpful to create a note-taking chart. Some possible charts might look like the following:

Questions to Establish Rapport	Responses/Answers

Grand Tour Questions	Responses/Answers

Task-Related Questions, to Meeting Challenges	Responses/Answers

Once students have gathered information and details, the next kind of composing to plan activity is to begin sketching out the plot and structure of the profile. By *plot* we mean to have students consider "what happens next" in the action they want to present in the article. In other words, what is the chronology of events? By *structure* we mean for students to think about the order in which they want to share the information and action. When we think about different structures to profile, we see several different possibilities.

Structure the profile as an epic story—a hero's journey. Tomas Alex Tizon (2007) writes that every profile should answer the question "Who is this person?" and that the "epic story is the larger narrative within which your subject's life fits" (72). This kind of structure is linear (event A followed by event B, etc.). The major values reflected in this kind of structure and story include determination, courage, luck, and other values that are associated with an "underdog" (Morgan 2003, 65).

Or another structure might be something like what Hart (2011) refers to as a "bookend narrative." In this kind of piece, there is a narrative opening and a return to the narrative at the ending. It might include the following elements:

- narrative opening that sets up the context (which includes the scene and the goal)
- a "promise" paragraph (or section) that tells the reader where the article is headed (this includes naming the goal and the complication that the person being profiled faces and is established and illustrated in the narrative opening)
- the background/history section that explains to readers the information that they need to know about the topic or the person or the issue in order to understand the rest of the piece
- the "keeping the promise" section that fulfills the promise laid out in the promise section
- the "to be sure" section (optional) that presents any alternate viewpoints and then refutes them from the profiled person's perspective
- the return to the narrative setup at the beginning of the piece to bring the reader full circle and have a sense of closure.

A third kind of structure might be one that alternates between scenes and information. Rather than being a linear structure, this can take a more modular design. That is, students can add as many "modules" of scenes or information that they like to create a sort of composite of the person being profiled (Bell 1997). For instance, writers might observe the person in multiple settings or at different times or with a range of people, and it may not all be structured in a chronological or linear way. It might look something like the following:

The idea in planning the skeleton of the piece is to help students begin to plan different chunks of the article by the purpose of that chunk. In other words, telling students here to "outline your details" is less helpful than encouraging them to think about *why* including details may help the reader in specific ways (e.g., creating a scene, providing information, creating background knowledge, etc.). These three structures are not the only kind of structures, and it would be helpful for students to inquire into the structure of other profiles (Fleischer and Andrew-Vaughan 2009; Lattimer 2003). In this kind of work, students could place an overhead transparency over a page of text and then draw boxes around different sections of the text. In those boxes on the transparencies, then, students could write the function or purpose of that section (e.g., introduce the character to the reader, present an alternate filter so that the writer could present how the profiled person might respond, etc.).

Early Draft Composing

In this phase of instruction, we provide opportunities for our students to try their hand at different parts of the magazine profile. When the task is challenging, as this one is, we will break down the larger piece into smaller chunks that are organized by function. That is, we want to help students figure out what they have in terms of facts, of scenes, and of commentary about the kinds of connections they see between their profiled person and the larger inquiry question and concepts that drive the unit of study.

In this first activity of this phase, we simply make sure that students lay out all the essential different pieces of information that they have collected and that they can relate these to the theme of meeting challenges. We ask students to begin drafting scenes that they want to include in the profile. You have a choice here to have students all begin with the same kind of scene (e.g., the opening scene, the ending scene, the pivotal or quintessential action scene for this person, etc.)

or you might have students choose to begin with a scene that they most want to include in the profile (or the scene that has the most energy for them).

After students have laid out the factual information they have collected and have written a scene or two, it is important to take some time to figure out what other data they might need to collect. This further collection of details might be through more observation, interviews, or outside resources (e.g., online, newspaper accounts, technical or business documentation, interviewing friends of the informant, etc.).

Final Draft Composing

In this phase of the instructional sequence, we help students move from their initial drafts to more complete and final drafts. For magazine profiles (and other kinds of narrative nonfiction), it is vital for students to track the scenes that are included in the pieces. The idea behind narrative nonfiction is that it is scene-based, so we like to have students use highlighters to note what they believe constitutes a scene in their writing (and in others' writing). If there is not much highlighting (i.e., scenes), then writers know that they have more revision and research to do.

Our instructional focus here is on seeing if students can name the different features of a magazine profile (declarative knowledge of form) and if they can describe how the features of a profile can be manipulated and used to highlight the message they want to share about their person (declarative knowledge of substance).

As students read their own work, we ask them to highlight what they see as scenes, what they see as exposition or summary (factual information they tell to the reader), and what they see as the place where they connect the profiled person's motivation up the ladder of abstraction to what others might think and believe about motivation. We might ask students the following questions:

- What do you notice as scenes in your article? (Please highlight the scenes.)
- What do you notice as exposition in your article? (Please use a different-color highlighter or put a box around the exposition.)
- Where do you move up the ladder of abstraction and connect this person's experience with larger ideas about challenges?

- What do you see as a particular strength of this draft?
- What one or two things would you most like other writers to help you consider before you revise?

As students read others' work, we ask them to first respond to the substance of the articles, and we might even start with the substance of the scenes. "What happens in the scene and are you able to follow the action clearly?" Then, we might ask students to respond to the big issues that writers identified as being most important to them. We like to use a PQP response, which stands for *praise* ("What works well?"), *question* ("What do you still wonder?"), *polish* ("What is the best bang for your buck move the writer could make in revising the piece?"). After our students identify the substance of the piece, we ask them to help one another think about shaping that substance. With a magazine profile and other kinds of narrative nonfiction, we might add one other kind of response to the PQP, which would be the C (PQCP), which stands for *connection*. Because narrative nonfiction, including a profile piece, asks for writers to move up the ladder of abstraction in a piece, we want to make sure writers receive feedback from others on the kinds of connections they are making to the story of the person being profiled. Sometimes we will ask students narrower questions, like "How is the profiled person's meeting of challenges like or unlike what is true for you? What scenes or information in the piece make you say this?"

One substantive problem our students often suffer from is telling instead of showing through a scene. We take some examples of telling from the students' writing or we generate some of our own. Then we model how to turn a telling comment into a showing scene. For example, we write "She is very animated," on the board, and then we think aloud as we write something like "Once at a party, she taunted her boyfriend: 'Catch me if you can!' as she kicked a bowl of buttered popcorn into his face and then climbed up on the roof, laughing like a baboon."

After modeling one, we have students do the next one together: Here's one we've used: "Tom is one of the most interesting and intelligent guys you will ever meet." Here's what some students came up with: "Tom veers his helicopter into tornado-like wind and lands on a tiny patch of snow in the middle of the Sawtooth Mountains. His Life Flight windbreaker flaps in the whipping wind." Students can then find sentences that need more specific showing detail in their own and in each others' writing and revise as needed.

➤ *Lesson idea*

For profiles, we find that it is important for students to learn how to use quotations, both for quoting the profilee and for quoting friends and others' responses in regard to the profiled person. We like to proceed inductively, by providing students with examples of different ways to integrate and punctuate quotes. We then ask small groups to induce the rules and finally to apply these rules to proofreading their own and each other's profiles. Here's a worksheet we have used:

Each item contains two sentences. The first is a quote that came from an interview. The second is a writer's citing that quote in a profile. Please read both sentences carefully, paying special attention to how they are punctuated. Then answer the questions that follow:

1. Quote: When the dust came swirling down the plains, it was like a giant tornado laying on its side and sucking everything up in sight.

   Profile sentence: When Mr. Jones reminisced about the giant dust storms he lived through as a boy; he recalled that one "was like a giant tornado lying on its side and sucking everything up in sight."

2. Quote: I knew from the moment I saw him that he was going to be causing me trouble.

   Profile sentence: Mr. Flynn faced many challenges in his first job, starting with his boss, who he knew right from the start "was going to be causing me trouble."

   What do you notice?

   What must you remember?

   What's the proofreading cue?

Composing to Transfer

At the end of the unit, we want to help students further articulate and consolidate their understandings, and we as teachers want to understand what students know about the purpose and contexts and processes of writing of magazine profiles. The most common and perhaps most revealing way to gauge students' understanding is to ask them to write a reflection. In the process of writing a reflection, we want them to point to specific moments during the writing process and to specific passages in their writing.

We ask students to create two different products. The first is simply a "writing process report," in which we give them the following prompts about their writing experience.

- How long did you spend on each stage of the writing process?
- What obstacles did you face as a writer and how did you overcome them?
- What resources did you use and which were the most helpful for you? (Resources might be people, texts, heuristics, conversations, etc.)
- What did you feel you did really well with the magazine profile?
- If you had more time or another shot at working on another magazine profile like this, what would you do differently process-wise, and what would you do differently in this particular magazine profile?
- What is it you would like me (teacher) to notice and to comment on as I respond to your writing?

In the second product, we want students to revisit the key concepts from the unit and connect them to their profile. To do this, we have students take their initial concept map (see previous activity) and then draw a second visual of how their profiled person might map those concepts. We ask them to compare the two maps, note their similarities and differences, and then present those to the rest of the class. As listeners, students must note any patterns or any gaps they notice across what others report.

Finally, we ask students to reflect on the content and write a short piece about what facing challenges and taking initiative means to them and to identify ways in which they could meet challenges in their lives, interest groups, families, school, or community in ways that would show initiative and some of the lessons gleaned from the writing and sharing of the profiles. We concluded by encouraging students to compose and commit to an action plan for meeting a challenge that made use of what they have learned.

We also want students to transfer the work they did as writers into their critical analyses of the world in which they live. Because the class has completed a collection of stories about overcoming challenges, students can begin to see how these stories shape and reflect a community's beliefs and values.

And once they've consider one collection of stories, they can move on to critically examine others. For example, we think it is useful and compelling for students to inquire into the ways stories about "young people" shape them. For instance, "What are the stories about teenagers/subgroups of teens that our society seems to share?" Oftentimes, these are stories of "raging hormones" or of being deficient in some way. Teenagers, the stories seem to say, need to be controlled. Or perhaps they want to investigate stories about being "rural" or "urban" or "suburban." Or maybe about "blue collar" or "middle class" or "privileged." Or so on.

For this analytical work, we turn to Lee Anne Bell (2010), who wrote a powerful book we hope and encourage you to read, *Storytelling for Social Justice*. In her work with inservice and preservice teachers, as well as with high school students, Bell and her colleagues focused on collections of stories about "race" and "racism." The question guiding this Storytelling Project Model work might be written in the following way: What do we lose when stories of and by diverse groups are concealed, silenced, or lost, and what do we gain as a society when we listen to and learn from the multitude of stories available for our consideration as we seek to dismantle racist structures and patterns in our society? (2010, 27). Bell's heuristic, like the one from Rymes (2009), is a strong one. She describes different kinds of stories that members of communities tell, though some are clearly more privileged and mainstream than others: stock stories, concealed stories, resistance stories, and emerging/transforming stories.

Bell describes each of these kinds of stories through her focus on race and racism in the following way:

- Stock stories: "Stock stories are the tales told by the dominant group, passed on through historical and literary documents, and celebrated through public rituals, law, the arts, education, and media" (Bell 2010, 23).

➤ *CCSS emphasis on different perspectives*

- Concealed stories: "Concealed stories reveal both the hidden (from the mainstream) stories told from the perspective of racially dominated groups . . . though invisible to those in the mainstream, concealed stories are circulated, told and retold by people in the margins whose experiences and aspirations they express and honor (Levins Morales 1998)" (Bell 2010, 23). The stock stories and the concealed stories are really two sides of the same coin, according to Bell, in that they each deal with the same events but only through the filters of different people and perspectives.

- Resistance stories: "These are the warehouse of stories that demonstrate how people have resisted racism, challenged the stock stories that support it, and fought for more equal and inclusive social arrangements throughout our history but seldom taught in our schools. Resistance stories include the reserve of stories accumulated over time about and by people and groups who have challenged an unjust racial status quo . . . Resistance stories teach about antiracist perspectives and practice that have existed throughout our history up to the present time to expand our vision of what is possible in our own antiracism work today" (Bell 2010, 24–25). Resistance stories serve as the foundation for emerging/transformative stories.

- Emerging/transformative stories: "These counter-stories are new stories deliberately constructed to challenge the stock stories, build on and amplify concealed and resistance stories, and create new stories to interrupt the status quo and energize change" (Bell 2010, 25). Some guiding questions Bell suggests include: "What would it look like if we transformed the stock stories? What can we draw from resistance stories to create new stories about what ought to be? What kinds of communities based on justice can we imagine and then work to enact? What kinds of stories can support our ability to speak out and act where instances of racism occur?" (Bell 2010, 26–27).

Clearly, these types of stories are connected to one another, but we think it provides a powerful framework for students and for us. We can't help but think about these kinds of stories in terms of our profession: What are the stock stories about teachers and teaching? What are the concealed stories? What are our resistance stories? What stories can we create to challenge and change the stock stories?

And think how these stories connect to any marginalized group or any group struggling for fuller civil rights—immigrants, migrant workers, the elderly, LGBT youth, those living in poverty, environmentalists, the Occupy Wall Street protesters, and many more. Focusing attention on such stories can lead to social action, social justice, and service learning.

Bell's book offers many more examples and iterations of this framework and model in action, but we present a glimpse of it here to highlight the ways in which we can help our students move beyond the CCSS' focus on composing narratives to a direction in which those compositions are embedded within big, important questions and connected to their lives and the change they hope to see in their communities.

Conclusion

Obviously, a unit such as the one on challenges we describe here could be organized around particular challenges from different times in history or around particular kinds of challenges that fit student interests or curricular demands. The important thing is that students delve deeply into the procedures of learning from others about what they have to offer on a compelling topic and that they learn how to frame what they have learned in a kind of story that will enlighten both the author of the piece and the reader while paying respect to the experience of their informant. These understandings and capacities will have a lifelong payoff.

CHAPTER 7

Writing Imaginative Narratives

But the imagination plays a far greater role in our lives than we customarily acknowledge, although any teacher can tell you how great an advocate the imagination is when a child is to be led into a changed course.

—Dorothea Brande

The three of us believe passionately in the power of imagination, and in the power of story to fuel and express imagination. In our methods courses and National Writing Project work, we endeavor to help the preservice and inservice teachers with whom we work to imagine new ways of being and working in their classrooms and schools. Some of the major questions that inform our teaching are: What if it were otherwise? I wonder what would happen if . . . ? How could we transform . . . ?

The central question of imagination is "What if?" What if-ness is a process of introducing something strange, unfamiliar, and perhaps even somewhat wild-eyed and demonstrably "outside the box" into our current situation or perspective.

Jim is currently imagining what it would look like to have his students work with Eli, a web service developed by his mentors and colleagues at the Writing in Digital Environments Research Center at Michigan State (www.elireview.com). It allows students to review one another's writing online, and then they are able to rate the reviews they receive from one another, which means Jim could see how students are making sense of one another's writing and one another's in-process feedback quickly enough that he could offer examples and minilessons right in the moment. Jim imagines how the classroom community might be different than what has developed in the past: How would students' relationships with one another and with their own writing process change if they were able to rate the feedback they received and offered one another? How might Jim's relationship with students change if he could offer them feedback on the feedback students offer one another? It's a different practice than what currently happens, and it's exciting to consider the possibilities.

Jeff is currently imagining how every unit he teaches could end with social action and service learning projects and what would happen if he did so. That is something new and unfamiliar to him, but he wants to build a classroom world where this will happen.

Michael is currently imagining how to devise a sequence of field experiences that will provide his preservice teachers opportunities to work with students of diverse linguistic and cultural backgrounds in a variety of school settings with mentor teachers who share his commitment to the kind of teaching we're talking about in this book. He realizes that in the past his imaginings have been limited by thinking too soon about what seems practical and believes that he has settled too quickly for what seems doable.

Imagination is a rehearsal for our future, for transformed being, for better, healthier, and more informed ways of living. We think imagination is vitally important to all teaching and learning, as well as to fulfilling personal growth and the development of more conjoint productive activities and democratic living.

The Power of Imaginative Narrative

Literary fiction, written and read, is engagement in what Santayana calls "imaginative rehearsals for living" (Booth 1983, 212)—for imagining how we would and should act in situations we haven't personally experienced to prepare ourselves for those (or similar) situations when we encounter them in the future.

Douglas Thomas and John Seely Brown, authors of *A New Culture of Learning* (2011a), have this to say:

> [C]reativity is the ability to use resources in new, clever, or unpredictable ways to solve a specific problem in a particular context. Creativity is *solution based*. In contrast, *imagination* is more of a preamble to a problem. Imagination allows us to ask the question "What if?" It allows us to imagine different

problems or different spaces to solve them. In the language of *A New Culture of Learning*, imagination is *inquiry based*. . . . The relationship between innovation and learning is about finding a relationship between what is familiar and what is strange. Creativity and imagination are both maps that allow us to do that. (2011b, 1; italics in original)

Thomas and Brown continue:

The *problem* is no longer one of finding a solution, but is instead a question of closing the gap between the familiar and the strange . . . What is critical, however, is that we understand that learning is a play between context and content, not the absence of one or the other. Imagination is as dependent on the familiar as it is on the strange in order to construct a "bounded learning environment." Imagination is at its most potent when it is tethered to a problem space that has real constraints, not only because it allows for focus but because it also provides a context to transform. Innovation is at its most powerful when it works through imagination. . . . Creativity alters content. Imagination reshapes context. (2011b, 1)

Given our approach to curriculum as inquiry, our argument that all composing must be contextualized in problem-based situations (bounded learning environments that require and reward specific kinds of learning and composing), and our assertion that the Common Core State Standards (CCSS) require imaginative use of what we have called "crux moves," both creativity and imagination are central to our project—but nowhere so obviously as when students read and compose imaginative narratives.

Imaginative narratives are acts of a storyteller's focusing others' gaze toward something unfamiliar and disruptive (a moment, a situation, a person, an exchange, etc.). And not just focusing a gaze, but focusing that gaze with a particular slant and through a particular filter, as we have discussed in earlier chapters. That is, when we think about why people tell stories, especially those they imagine, we think it is largely because people want others to notice something and consider something new, unfamiliar, perhaps jolting. Telling imaginary stories, therefore,

are acts of authority. Richard Ford (2007) writes about this in his introduction to
in *The New Granta Book of the American Short Story*. Ford writes:

> By authority I mean, roughly speaking, a writer's determina-
> tion, variously enacted, to assume provisional command of a
> reader's attention and volition, thereby overcoming a reader's
> resistance and engaging his credulity for the purpose of inter-
> posing some scheme the writer imagines to be worth both his
> and the reader's time and trouble. (xiii–xv)

Composing to Plan: Developing Knowledge of Purpose and Context

What's worth a reader's and writer's time? Our answer throughout the books of
our series has been "A text that addresses a question that matters in some compelling way." That's why we embedded our work on "stories of the self" in a unit
that addresses the question "What makes me, me?" That's why we embedded our
work on profiles in a unit that addresses the question "How do people meet challenges?" That's why we embed the work we're suggesting on fictional narratives
in what we feel is an equally compelling question: "What does it mean to cope
with loss in a healthy way?"

But before we ask students to take up that question, we want them to think
hard about the place of stories in their lives. When we first introduce the idea
of composing imaginative stories, students are already somewhat familiar with
what they will be asked to do: "Make up stuff," as one of Jim's former seventh
grade students put it. Making up stuff is fun. And it's challenging to do well. Less
clear are why people decide to make up stuff and then share it with others and
why those other people might enjoy it. As we begin working with students, we
want to provide lots of opportunities for students to practice and plan stories
they might decide to pursue for an extended period of time, and we want to do
so within an immediate context of use. In other words, we aim for our students
to be strategic, independent, and savvy when crafting imaginative stories in our
classes, so that they can do so in this and other contexts and for a wide range of
articulated purposes.

With this aim in mind, we spend some time working with students to consider all the places and all the occasions and all the attendant purposes where
people create and share imaginative stories with one another to help students
locate possible purposes. An anchor chart (a Where, When, Why chart) on the
wall or an online space would look like this:

Where Do You See Imaginative Stories? (Where Do You Find Made-up Stories?)	When Do You See Imaginative Stories?	Based on the Where and When, Why Do You Think People Are Sharing Those Imaginative Stories?
On television	At night	To make people laugh and to sell some products
Around the campfire	When camping	To scare or spook one another, to provide a thrill, to demonstrate skill in storytelling, to create a shared experience and feeling of camaraderie
In picture books	When a parent is reading it to a child	To soothe and reassure, to help the child go to sleep, or to help the child learn a lesson of some kind
On the Internet, like the Onion site	Daily, like a traditional newspaper	To point out the absurdities in events that are reported in more traditional news outlets, to add a new perspective beyond the traditional
In tabloids	At the grocery story	To circulate gossip and the fanciful, to entertain
When getting together with friends and family	Around the kitchen table or in the living room	To identify oneself, to entertain, to share a laugh, to provide hypotheticals and a context for getting advice or guidance
In problematic personal disputes or problems	Explaining why you didn't do what your friend asked you to do; explaining how you missed picking up your friend after school	To help your friend imagine why you acted the way that you did
In problematic professional situations—when faced with a really hard problem to solve	At the doctor's office, in a classroom	To imagine what might be the cause of a rare disease or how to solve a problem during surgery: What if . . .? To imagine what kind of instruction might help students through a difficulty: What if . . .?

After creating a chart like this (we'd keep it up in the room or active in our online space), we ask students to find patterns in each column and in the kind of connections within each row. For example, we would ask students, "What do you see as the similarities between each of the contexts where you find make-believe stories? Do any of the contexts seem different than the rest? How so?" We would ask similar questions for each of the columns. As we look at the pattern in the last column, we see a common purpose of storytellers wanting to point out something to an audience, to get them to notice something, such as the importance of a product, the unknown but entirely justifiable reason you didn't pick up a friend, new angles of thinking through and solving a problem, and so on.

We would also ask students to name the relationship between each of the columns for each row. For instance, in the row above focused on television stories, we see the context being connected to a time when many people are watching the same stories. And we see the connection between the place and time of the storytelling exchange being connected to the purposes of entertaining and selling, because it follows that advertisers and television people want as many people to see their stories as possible. It's good for business. Being engaging, surprising, worthy of being talked about all helps to get the message out.

This is a slightly different relationship between time/place and purpose that we find in other rows. The campfire stories, for example, are more about bringing people together through a shared experience. Put another way, campfire storytellers are swapping stories with one another, because the stories bring them together. It's fun. It's vital to make the group be a group.

In this kind of activity students are heightening their awareness about where, when, and why people tell stories that they create from their imaginations. This develops knowledge of context and purpose and gets kids started on composing to practice and plan. We also ask students to consider the content of what is being shared in these kinds of stories. In other words, not only do we look at the *where*, *when*, and *why* of the storytelling exchange, we also look at *what* is being shared, because doing so sheds some light on the purpose and the context of sharing imaginative stories too. This also serves to link our activities helping students develop knowledge of the purpose and contexts of imaginative fiction to activities helping students develop knowledge about the form and substance of such stories.

With this preparation, we turn to our inquiry question: "What does it mean to cope with loss in a healthy way?" We ask this question because we know and see people dealing with loss daily. Sometimes this loss is big—like with death and disease—sometimes the loss is less lasting—like losing one's keys or wallet. As educators, we see people dealing with loss all the time—a loss of innocence, a loss of trust in others, a loss of who they thought they were before they entered our courses, a loss of friendships, a loss of a pet, and so on. In this sequence, we want our students to deal with the concepts of loss, grief, change, and health, and we will ask them to write short pieces of literary fiction to create characters and situations that respond or react to loss in a variety of ways, ranging from unhealthy to healthy.

While the Where, When, Why chart helps our students think about the purposes and contexts of imaginative narratives, we also want them to begin thinking about the purposes and contexts of grieving and healing and how that might look like a process they can see people experiencing in a variety of ways in daily lives. We know that this creates potential for students to develop compassion or at least understanding of why some people and characters respond the way they do (see Wilhelm and Novak 2011). The activity here is one Jim has dubbed "Define CCR," in honor of one of his dad's favorite bands.

It looks like this:

Define: What is *X*? What are *X*'s essential features?

Compare: How is *X* like and unlike _____?

Change: How and why does *X* change?

Relationship: How and why is *X* linked to _____?

For our sequence on dealing with loss, this heuristic might look like:

- What is loss? What are the essential traits and processes of loss?
- How might loss involve grief or sorrow? How is grief like and unlike sorrow, like losing a game, like a physical injury? How might loss lead to new opportunities?
- How and why does loss change, evolve, get processed?
- How and why is loss linked to a person's health, to their outlook, to how they meet future challenges?

After we have individual students jot down their initial ideas in response to these questions, we ask them to slowly build up and share their ideas with others, first with a partner, then with a group of four. As they work in small groups of four, they must create a document to share and post in the classroom. Once we have the ideas about grieving posted throughout the room, we ask students to look for patterns or outliers across the group's responses. "What do you see that's the same?" we ask. "Where is something that's not like the rest?" Students take notes as they take a gallery walk around the room to sort and identify patterns and outliers. In short, we're asking students to take up the question Ford suggests, "What's worth a reader's and writer's time?" What about loss do students want their readers to notice and contend with?

Composing to Practice: Producing the Substance of Characters and Storyworlds

When we ask students to create stories, we know that some of our students will feel anxious and sometimes frozen. Creating a story, like any creative act, takes a certain element of courage, and we would be remiss not to mention the emotions our students face when engaging in the writing of a short story (see Ralph Keyes [1995] *The Courage to Write* for an extended and thoughtful look at how more experienced writers deal with fear). With this in mind, we want to provide our students with many, many possible stories to follow in a more extended way. Because of this, we ask our students to collect characters and storyworlds, because these are the two most common ways into a story and because doing so gives them a rich set of possibilities to draw on when they compose their own stories.

We also know that there is a paradox to creating and composing imaginative narratives. "How much do you have to know about what you want to say before you say it?" is a valid question in classrooms when writers try to write stories. We know that we want students to discover and be surprised by their characters, but we also know that there is a deadline to projects produced in class—and out in the world (like this book!). Put another way, when we have students read stories, we generally ask them two big questions, "What does the writer want you to notice?" ("How do you know?" is a helpful follow-up question) and "What do you think that means?" This is an observation-interpretation pattern to responding to the narratives we read. To promote reading like a writer, we further ask students:

"What did you notice that you'd like to try in your story?" and "What ideas does this stimulate for your story?"

We get off the dime by reading various stories that help us explore the conceptual theme of the inquiry about loss. As we do so, we can help students explore the concept and also different rhetorical moves that storywriters make to help readers experience stories of loss and to create effects and meanings surrounding the theme.

We like to start with picture books, and in this unit we have used Kalman's (2002) *Fireboat*, which deals with 9/11 and starts with a sense of setting and era; *The Journey*, about Japanese internment that deals with loss of home and identity and civil rights; Murphy's *George Washington and the General's Dog* (2002), which deals with General Howe's lost dog, which was returned to him by his enemy George Washington and displays how to gradually reveal secrets in a story, and many others. Depending on the age of our students, we might move from these children's books to other stories. Among those we have used are John Steinbeck's "Flight," John Updike's "Ace in the Hole," Willa Cather's "Paul's Case," James Baldwin's "Sonny's Blues," and Carson McCullers' "A Rock, a Tree, a Cloud." We ask students both to analyze and to write from these readings.

➤ *Lesson idea*

For "Flight," we asked students to choose a good description that was particularly effective at creating setting, and then to write after this model. We also asked them to find objects that recur in the story and to discuss how these contributed to story meaning.

For "Paul's Case," we ask students to identify the external and internal conflicts of Paul and how Cather shows these. We then ask students to list the external and internal conflicts they have experienced around loss. Students practice showing some of these conflicts instead of just telling what they are, following the models of Cather.

For "Ace in the Hole," we ask students to describe the character of Ace and what he has lost throughout the story. We ask how Updike shows Ace's character and how we use these cues to create a sense of him. We then ask them to imagine other details that might deepen their understanding of Ace. We repeat this process with Ace's wife and young child. We conclude with an examination of how the loss and the ways of dealing with it are affected by the characters' values.

Baldwin's "Sonny's Blues" is great for getting at point of view, perspective, filter, and slant. We ask students to rewrite a scene through Sonny's filter, to share how they have done so, and to consider how this changes meaning and effect. We focus on how perspective is revealed and shown through subtle cues.

Well, you get the idea: With each story, we use the opportunity to discuss loss, what led to the loss, how characters deal with it, and what lesson or theme is expressed about dealing with loss through all of this. We also use each text as a mentor text to get ideas about both content and form for our own stories—using the stories to practice developing procedural knowledge of substance and form. In so doing, we are not only preparing students to write their own stories, this is working toward writing anchor standard 3, we are also helping to meet CCSS reading standards on key ideas and details and on craft and structure.

➤ *Reading anchor standards 1–6*

When we ask students to write stories, they often want to start with what they want their stories to mean (the interpretation), before they've considered what their character wants and what the character believes is at stake (the observations). So we want to provide multiple opportunities for students to consider and create a wide range of characters and storyworlds before beginning to pursue one character's story. This seems to short-circuit any temptation to interpret before creating the story. It's only after students have created their character and storyworld, and only after they have begun putting that character in motion, that we will return to the larger question, "What does this character's experience make us notice about the way people respond to loss? Is that a healthy response? If so, how? If not, why did this response seem like the right one to the character? What beliefs would the character have to change to respond in a different, healthier way?" If we were to ask these questions early in the writing process, students would be too focused on what the story "means" rather than on the narrative experience and power of discovery that comes from following the character through the events she faces.

➤ *Lesson idea*

We begin by helping students consider the WAGS test when collecting characters, an activity we describe in some detail in Chapter 3. As a reminder, we want students to think about potential worlds for a character, actions a character might take, a primary goal the character might have, and the stakes for the character in reaching or not reaching that goal. To get students playing with this heuristic, we use several techniques.

➤ *Lesson idea*

We use images to create and collect characters from online sources, magazines, paintings, advertisements, photographs, and more. For instance, Google has archived photos from *Life* magazine at http://images.google.com/hosted/

life and *National Geographic* hosts its photographs at http://photography.nation-algeographic.com/photography/. When we use these sources, we can show image after image on the screen while students use the images as triggers to get them started on the WAGS test. In a more logistical sense, before we have students begin, we have them write *WAGS* down the side of a sheet of paper (or in a Word document) so that they can simply riff on the page when we have images resting on the LCD screen in our classrooms.

As students view the portraits, they can infer character and practice the WAGS by answering questions such as these:

- World: What is this character's typical setting? Favorite hangout? What does their room look like at home?

- Action: What are their favorite activities? Job? Favorite Friday night fun? Hobbies?

- Goals: What does this character most want? What are the obstacles to achieving it?

- Stakes: What are the stakes involved in achieving the goal, or not achieving it?

In an activity called Picture Talk, students can set the character from one photograph into conversation with another one using the following prompts derived from WAGS:

- World: Where might these two people be likely to meet?

- Action: What might be a mutual action or interest they would undertake together, or an issue they might have a dispute about?

- What does the first person say to the second to start the conversation? How does content and language reveal character?

- What does the second character say in response?

This process can be continued and offers an opportunity for students to create and play with characters, invent conflicts, write and punctuate scripts or dialogue, and much more. A third person can be introduced into the scene as needed.

Sometimes students are unable to complete all the WAGS items for all the characters, but that's OK by us. The idea here is that they are collecting characters they may potentially follow in a story. Our aim is to just generate possibilities, and by having students collect many characters, potential story ideas can germinate (or marinate, if you prefer) over time.

➤ Lesson idea

We also use images to create and collect storyworlds from the same kind of visual sources. We might show landscape scenes or scenes from everyday life or of urban or rural settings, and then ask our students, "What person wants to be there, but isn't?" and "What person is stuck there, but can't leave?" This begins to help students generate ideas about the constraints people face, and they begin to build rules and relationships between people and the space. We have students do this multiple times, and we have them share and share some more with one another so that they have many possible characters and storyworlds to choose from.

➤ Lesson idea

In addition to collecting characters and storyworlds through the use of images, we also use old phone books, catalogs, and brochures as ways to create and collect characters and storyworlds. For instance, when using old phone books, we say that a student cannot use a person's name in its entirety; instead, they must mix and match names. Once they have a name for a character, then we have them create a character using the WAGS test. We later ask students what the name reveals or suggests about the character so that they see how authorial decisions about names, other details, expression, and craft make a difference to the readers' experience and to meaning. We also have students take the names of businesses or of streets and then ask the same questions about storyworlds: "Who wants to be there, but can't?" and "Who wants to leave there, but can't?" We also have students mix and match any images they might see in advertisements in any of those kinds of texts. Students describe the physical details without making any judgments. "What do you see?" is the question students must respond to. No interpretations. Then, after they list concrete details, we ask them to put characters in the space to interact with the set pieces in the scene.

➤ Lesson idea

The idea in these sorts of assignments is to start small and without much at stake, so that writers can have ideas to choose from. Ray Bradbury does something similar that we sometimes ask our students to try. Bradbury creates long list of images after images, and then after creating the list, he looks for patterns (Koch 2003). For our students, we might guide them a bit. We might ask them to create a list of images (or to collect such images online) you might see at a circus. Or at a zoo, a mall, a bus stop, a subway station, a rodeo, a basketball game, a place of worship, and so on. After a list of ten to twenty images, we have students share by posting the ideas (online or across the room), allowing students to add to each other's and their own lists of striking images. Once they have a fairly strong list, we then ask them to see if they can find any patterns that lead to a particular slant. For example, are there patterns in the list of images that suggest fun, humor, happiness, twistedness, creepiness, playfulness, wonder? We then ask students to create at least three characters who might view this place with one of those slants that seem to fit a pattern from the images.

➤ *CCSS on pattern seeking and inferencing, multimodal composing, and so on*

After students have created characters—with a goal and stakes—we ask them to write a few different quick moments the character experiences. Here's a quick summary of what we ask them to do:

- First, write for (three minutes, one hundred words, etc.) about this character being lost in this unfamiliar place. Students have to include at least three of the images from their collection (or from any of the shared collections).
- Second, write for (three minutes, one hundred words, etc.) with this character receiving some bad, even shocking or weird news, from a stranger who doesn't know that it's bad news for your character.
- Third, write for (three minutes, one hundred words, etc.) with the character taking an uncharacteristic action, behaving in an uncharacteristic way, or being angry at another character without saying anything negative to this character.

After each round, we provide all students some time to share with one another in pairs or triads, as partners ask one another, "What do you think will happen next?"

Our hope in this composing to practice phase is to provide many opportunities to create multiple characters, storyworlds, actions, stakes, and situations that could be extended into at least a couple of scenes. Because we are asking students larger questions about people's grieving, we know that we want to create scenes that establish what a character wants, that show the character experiencing a loss, and that show how the character responds to that loss. This could be accomplished in one scene or in multiple scenes, and depending on the needs of our students, we would adjust accordingly. We think it is helpful and important to have students create at least two scenes to show a change over time or a change in different locations.

Composing to Practice and to Plan: Shaping Scenes to Develop Knowledge of Substance and Form

We hope that we've created multiple opportunities for students to create many characters, storyworlds, and situations that they can choose to extend into a longer piece. When they choose, students should pick a character they want to follow. That is, students should ask themselves, "Do I know exactly what's going to happen to this character?" If so, it's probably a good idea to not pursue that character's story. Instead, we think it's helpful for students to pursue a character whose story is still a kind of a mystery to them. As writing teachers, we want our students to see that writing can be an act of discovery—that not all writing occasions are about recording what you already know in your head. Instead, sometimes—maybe even many times—we can have questions and through the process of writing we can begin to discover the answers. We think story writing is one of those opportunities. After all, story writing is about imagining the as yet unknown.

When we have students begin to shape their characters, storyworlds, and situations into more extended pieces, we ask them to begin with the moment that most interests them. From there, students work with a linear design, thinking about complications and resolutions to a couple of scenes.

➤ *Lesson idea*

More specifically, here's what we've asked students in middle school to do:

1. Take a look at all the characters they have collected. In the margins, students rate them on a scale from 1 to 10, with 1 being the least interesting and 10 being the most interesting. You decide what "interesting" means to you, though it is probably someone who is going to introduce something new, unfamiliar, and strange into the storyworld. Share your two most interesting characters with a thinking partner.

2. Now go back to the two characters who seem the most interesting and write down what questions you want to ask about their lives.

3. List at least five or six questions that capture what strikes your curiosity the most.

After writing down their own questions about their own characters, students circulate around the room. As each student shares with another, the listener must provide one question about the writer's character that they want answered. So, for instance, if Jim has created a character and a list of questions that he is interested in figuring out, he would share it with Michael. Michael would then tell Jim what he's curious to learn about Jim's character. Jim would then record the question, and then circulate around the class some more and repeat the process with another person, like Jeff, who would ask a trenchant and stimulating question that Jim would then record. (In this unit, we might suggest students ask a general question and also a more specific one about the character's relationship to loss or grief.)

After students have a list of questions about their characters, they can then rate those questions from least compelling to most compelling. Once they have a question they find most compelling, then the challenge is to figure out how to create a scene that answers that question. Students might begin with either a complication or a resolution, and our work is to help them take where they are starting and move to the other. For example, in Jim's story about Mr. O'Conner and Amanda, one question Jim wondered about Mr. O'Conner was, what happens when he can talk about why he's feeling lonely? Jim wanted to see how that might play out, so he had to work backward to figure out a way to create a moment that allowed him to share with another person. Enter Amanda, his teenage neighbor who also feels lonely. The challenge as a writer was figuring out how to put them in conversation with one another so that they could talk about how they felt and show how they were each grieving.

For students, the temptation is simply to answer the questions they have by just telling and without dramatizing. That is, they want to merely state or declare rather than show what happens. This is not necessarily a bad place to begin, but clearly it won't lead to a narrative nor dramatic scene. If students are simply reporting what happens, we acknowledge what students have written, but then we might ask them to craft a scene with only dialogue. After doing so, then we ask them to put the reporting (the exposition) with the dialogue, and later find moments where they can add set pieces from the storyworld and thoughts from the character who is our filter.

Other times, students might have trouble connecting their characters to our inquiry question or to a subquestion of it (e.g., "What does it mean to cope with loss in a healthy way?"). When this happens, we ask students to take the compelling character they want to follow and work through multiple filters that can

➤ *Lesson idea*

reveal how a character is feeling. For this sequence on dealing with loss (or "griev-ing"), we adapt this activity from Denise Gess (Ellis 2009). We first ask students to write a couple of paragraphs that describe their character looking at a physical location (e.g., if the character is in a park, then the character is describing what she or he sees in the park). Then students rewrite those two paragraphs as though the character is experiencing each of the five stages of grief. In other words, we say, "Rewrite those two paragraphs as though the character is in denial." Then, "Rewrite those two paragraphs as though the character is angry." And students continue rewriting the setting description though each of the five stages of de-nial, anger, depression, resignation, and acceptance (Kübler-Ross 1969). We like to remind students to use details about the lighting, the sounds, and smell to cre-ate a specific kind of atmosphere. (See "Moody Words" activity from Smith and Wilhelm 2010).

This kind of practice helps students in multiple ways. One, it is focused on a particular kind of story writing problem: How do things look to the character who is feeling a specific kind of emotion? Two, how does this description help to illustrate the character's response, perspective, and feelings and to set up the character's next actions? That is, students can use one of these rewrites as a way to dramatize the character's response. Three, the multiple rewrites offer students multiple possibilities about what comes before or after this moment. In other words, students can discover something about the character and then students can make a decision about a complication or resolution (or both) based on mul-tiple possibilities they tried during the rewrites.

➤ *Lesson idea*

Once students have one compelling moment drafted, we then work on hav-ing students use a complication–resolution framework to create a series of cause–effect moments. We should note that we head students in both directions. That is, we want to know the series of causes and effects that led up to this moment, as well as the series of causes and effects that follow this moment. It might look like this in a graphic:

Cause → Effect leads to Cause → Effect leads to THIS
MOMENT leads to Cause → Effect leads to Cause → Effect

Another way of writing this might be using the language of complication and resolution.

Complication → Response/Resolution leads to Complication → Response/Resolution leads to THIS MOMENT leads to Further Complication → Response/Resolution leads to further Complication → Resolution

This is a kind of timeline that is more than just a list of events, but rather a list of connected events, or as the CCSS might call it, an "event sequence." In creating this chain of cause–effects or complications–response/resolutions, students are able to make visible multiple events, and then they are able to choose where they may want to begin or end the story. That is, they are mapping out the plot of this character's story, though the students will not know exactly what will happen to each of the characters in those moments. Things might change as students write, but this timeline with connected events can help students put boundaries around the events they want to share with readers.

During this phase of instruction when we are focused on students beginning to pursue and shape a character's story, we make sure that students continue to consider the character's goals and motivations, even if the character is unaware of what she or he wants or needs. We mean this in terms of the entire story—what are the character's big goals and why do these matter to the character?—but more immediately, we are focused on what the character wants and why the character believes the stakes are high within the immediate scene.

When characters are faced with complications in pursuing these important goals within a scene, then we see the character responding, which creates a next action, a new complication. It propels the story forward. Because we are focused on characters responding to loss, we have to make sure our students are creating characters who face complications that make them lose something—an idea, an emotion, an object, a state of being or status, and so on. We're not ready yet, at this phase of the process, to ask students, "What do you want your readers to notice about how people respond to loss?" because that's too much interpretation too soon. Instead, we are helping students create compelling characters who are faced with moments where changes are possible and a loss can occur.

As students engage in this kind of work, they explore wide notions of loss together and imaginatively rehearse different responses including different kinds of grieving. This builds understanding of the self and of others at the same time that they are learning the principles behind how to compose and read imaginative narratives in general transferable ways, as well as how to meet specific CCSS standards for composing and understanding event sequences, characters, perspectives and much else.

It's in this phase of instruction that we help students make sense of different text-specific genre demands for other kinds of imaginative narratives. For example, if we were asking students to write what is typically called "genre fiction" (e.g., romance, mystery, sci-fi, fantasy), then we would concentrate here on how to shape characters and storyworlds into forms that are recognizable to others as those kinds of stories. So we'd look specifically at creating romantic heroines and heroes, romantically motivated storyworlds and actions, goals and stakes.

Similarly, if we were asking students to create a script, a fairy tale, a myth, a legend, or other kinds of imaginative narratives, we would work here in the same way of supporting students' understanding of what others expect and recognize with these specific kinds of imaginative narratives (e.g., in romance: the complication being the separation of potentially romantic partners either psychologically and/or physically, the heroine's reform of the hero, the hero's realization of the heroine's worth and the worth of her vision, the reconciliation amid deeper awareness, the integration of interests and recognition of the full personhood of each other, etc.).

Early Draft Composing: Putting Characters in Motion

At this point in the process, students have multiple characters, storyworlds, and situations to work with, and we think they have begun not only to pursue a character's story but to sketch out a compelling scene and series of events around that scene. In some courses, we might only have our students work with different kinds of scenes. For instance, we might have them create a portfolio of scenes that reveal a range of characters responding to similar situations in different ways. For example, students might create multiple scenes that show a handful of their collected characters responding to a mutual loss or different losses (the loss of a team member, or different losses of family or friends on 9/11). This can lead to a more modular design of a final artifact, and it can help us see how students create and combine the building blocks of story (declarative and procedural knowledge of form) and understand people responding to loss in a variety of ways (declarative and procedural knowledge of substance). We might even have students rate or organize those characters in their scenes from least to most healthy in their dealings with loss as a way to see what our students understand about the key concepts of the unit.

In this sequence, however, we're interested in our students being able to link a series of events, so we employ a more linear design to the stories as a way to help us see what students understand and can do with chronology and with cause/effect ways of thinking.

At this point of the process, sometimes students want to abandon the character or the character's situation they have been working with. Because we have done a lot of work creating multiple possibilities and multiple opportunities to engage in the process, we are less worried about students heading in a new direction than if we hadn't done this work. They should have achieved deep and transferable understandings and productive strategies for producing new material. This is in fact the test of the effectiveness of our method.

We use this kind of moment to explore what our students understand about narratives as well as about loss. We ask them questions about characters' goals and stakes, and we wonder how they might change those goals or stakes to make a piece more compelling, interesting, unfamiliar, or challenging to themselves and a reader. *Or*, if they are tired of the character, we might ask them what other character they might want to follow that would make things more compelling for themselves and their readers. If students have good reasons that use their understanding of narrative principles, then we feel comfortable letting them move forward in a new direction, because they can explain what isn't working and how they might alter things so that it can work.

Final Draft Composing: Helping Readers

We want to help students revise at a few different levels as they create final drafts. These levels include: the word level, the sentence level, and the whole-text level.

At the word level, we ask students to work with the conventions of dialogue. We work here in a few different ways. One way is to concentrate on the use of commas and other punctuation around dialogue and dialogue tags. Dialogue tags are things like "said" or "asked" or "wondered." We work a lot with tags in that we pretty much ask our students to only use variations of "say" rather than a whole long list of other tags that we sometimes see. We think these range of tags are actually distracting when we read stories, and they also are shortcuts to making writing more lively and vivid. That is, we want students to use these tags as ways to tell readers what a character sounds like, rather than using other techniques like the use of silence or gestures or repetition of words as a way to show the emotion a character is experiencing as she or he speaks.

Helping students write dialogue provides an opportunity to see how the five kinds of knowledge and composing are at play even when students learn strategies and conventions.

INQUIRY SQUARE FOR DIALOGUE

	Declarative	Procedural
Form	Quotation marks around speakers' words and end punctuation Tag lines at beginning, middle, or end of speaking New paragraph (indent) every time speakers change	How do we help kids practice using the correct conventions? • Provide models • Apply rules to borrowed dialogue • Write notes back and forth and then transfer it to a dialogue • Use kinesthetic mystery plot • Produce a dialogue together and punctuate it together • Practice editing own work for punctuation and tag lines
Substance	Tag lines: should reveal emotion, subtext Quote: be substantive, move things forward, revealing Voice: should be dramatic, reveal character, dialect Substance: talk should matter/be about something, reveal character	How can we make it happen? Practice generating dialogue by: • Dramatizing a scene or problem • Role-playing • Using scenarios • Using picture talk activity • Stepping into the picture activity • Filling in missing dialogue in a cartoon, filling in some of the missing dialogue • Turning the volume down on a video and students providing the dialogue
Purpose	To reveal character, and further plot, provide background information in a way that is lively to read and contextualized in human interactions Create and intensify conflict, use multiple voices and perspectives, eliminate texture and streamline the writing, dramatize interaction, show vs. tell	

At the sentence level, we ask students to play with different sentence structures, particularly those that help students move their readers from what they already know to what is not yet known. For example, we work with students on dividing sentences into two parts: what comes before the verb and what follows the verb. We show students how what comes before the verb refers to the ideas or key words used at the end of the previous sentence, and then we show students how the end of each sentence is a power position, because it offers new information that we want the readers to remember.

At the whole-text level, we ask students to read one another's work to see if they can follow the logic of the story. Do complications and resolutions lead to the next complications and resolutions? Do we know what the character wanted and why it mattered to the character? Have peer editors retell the complication-response and their emotional engagement at each phase. Discuss ways to intensify or to highlight important moves in dealing with loss.

Composing to Transfer: Naming What We've Learned and Still Wonder About

At the end of this sequence, we're interested in knowing what our students understand about narrative and what they understand about dealing with loss (our unit's key conceptual center). To help them name what they understand and how they understand it, and to help us see and help to name and celebrate what they understand, we ask them to compose in a few different ways.

One, we ask them to write a paragraph or two about what they believe their character reveals about how people deal with loss. Then students post these paragraphs for other students to read. Students are asked to read multiple paragraphs, taking notes about what people seem to be saying about the various means for dealing with loss, in both less and more healthy ways, necessary and unnecessary ways. Once students have collected their thoughts and notes from a variety of paragraphs, they write a two-sentence summary of their findings. The first begins with this sentence starter, "Our class seems to generally believe that healthy dealing with loss is _____." The second begins with this starter, "I (dis)agree, based on _____." This gives us a sense of what each student thinks about the

➤ Lesson idea

larger inquiry question, and it gives us a sense of how they are reading other people's thinking.

➤ *Lesson idea*

Two, we ask students to tell us the story of writing their story. (See our discussion of process analysis in Wilhelm, Smith, and Fredricksen 2012.) We want to know what students wanted to have happen as they wrote, what complications they faced as writers, what resources helped in facing those complications, and what they will do similarly and what they will do differently the next time they create a story. This helps us get a sense of what students understand about themselves as writers and what they understand about composing narratives.

➤ *Lesson idea*

Three, we ask students to create a concept map of the key concepts in this unit, which includes loss, grief, change, and health, and extend the map to all other concepts that these relate to. We want to know how our students see these concepts as being connected to one another. Then, we ask them to draw another map from their character's filter. How does their character see the relationship between these things? We then ask them to write about what happens in the story that makes them think their character sees things this way, and we ask them to compare their maps to their character's maps. Sometimes the maps will be the same. Sometimes they will be different. Either way, it opens up a discussion about how imaginative narratives help writers get their readers to notice specific ideas, responses, characters, and more (as well as the difference between author, narrator, and character).

In other words, we think this discussion helps our students see connections between the characters they imagined with life outside the world of their stories. It opens up possibilities for our students to understand how fictional characters help us dramatize that which we notice and wonder about in our own lives. That's a good and hopeful thing. It's a step in the processes of transforming the self and transforming the world. And those are two worthy goals we work hard for and that imaginative storytelling helps us to reach.

CHAPTER 8

Composing Narratives with Words and Images

*Words and pictures are yin and yang. Married, they produce
a progeny more interesting than either parent.*

—Ted Geisel (aka Dr. Seuss)

Visualizing is essential to creating and experiencing narratives as a reader and as a writer. And many narratives involve or are based on visuals: whether expressed through slide shows, movies, YouTube videos, websites, artwork, photography, and so on.

Last fall, Jim was working in Emily Morgan's classroom of English language learners as some of the students were trying to understand *Romeo and Juliet*. One ninth-grade boy was intrigued by the class' discussion about healthy relationships that framed the reading, yet, like many ninth graders, he was struggling to follow each of the characters and how they were related to one another. However, when the student began reading the graphic novel version, as well as "reading" the different film versions of various scenes in the story, he was able to visualize the story, which helped him see how characters were related to one another (and much more).

A lot of Jeff's research (Wilhelm 2008, 2004) focuses on (1) how essential visualization is to both reading and composing, and (2) how struggling readers and writers can be helped through the use of visual strategies and supports. It's so important that the title of one of Jeff's books is *Reading Is Seeing* (2004). Jeff's research has also documented how visual strategies are particularly engaging for struggling students. In his recent teaching of refugee children, he has found that using graphic novels and visuals gives these students an immediate way to be successful, helps them to become part of the classroom project by contributing significantly to it, and provides a bridge toward more conventional English and composing activities.

One of Michael's family's favorite activities is to gather around the hundreds of family photos (someday he'll get them in albums) and pick through them, telling the story that occasioned the picture as they do so. It's been a great way for Michael's granddaughter to learn her family's history, and now she's an eager participant with her own photos. And she's become an accomplished storyteller in her own right. Our experience both in and out of school confirms the importance of being able to tell stories with both words and images. Given the growing importance of image in popular cultural literacies, you'd think that students would immediately embrace working on such stories. But that's not always the case

Why Compose with Visual Media and Multimodalities?

"Why are we writing comics? I thought we were writing essays," the high school student challenges his teacher, Mitch Nobis. The student is in his twelfth-grade composition class and had figured out the rules to the game of school long ago. It's this kind of student, rather than the struggling student, who most resists working with words and images. Nobis knows and has experienced this resistance since he began working with comics, graphic novels, and other visual texts years ago.

Nobis responds to the student, "For a few reasons. . . ." A teacher at Seaholm High School and Co-Director of the Red Cedar Writing Project, Nobis explains to this student that not only is creating comics fun and different but it will actually help in writing essays and other more academic arguments and informational texts for two reasons: (1) these texts involve visuals and are often presented visually, and (2) making rhetorical choices for audiences and purposes more visual and concrete helps to both develop and transfer sophisticated skills to more traditional writing. Moreover, he argues that teaching and learning visual literacy matters because these texts are valuable in and of themselves. As the philosopher Charles Sanders Pierce argues: The world is a profusion of symbols and signs. Katie Wood Ray (2011) explains how they interact in picture books:

By looking closely at the decisions illustrators make in picture books, teachers can help children understand many of the most important concepts about quality writing. Illustrators make meaning with pictures, and writers make meaning with words, but they both *make meaning*, and rich curriculum lies in understanding all the ways their decisions intersect. The key is, in order to help students grow as writers, teachers need a deeply grounded understanding of the ways thinking about writing and thinking about illustrating are the same. This, however, is very new thinking for many teachers—myself included. (72)

In our terms, both making meaning in words and with images, or combinations, are profound acts of *composing*.

Students need to compose with both words and images because it is how we all make meaning. Of course, one challenge is figuring out how to do so in a way that supports and develops students' understanding of composing processes, of narrative principles and genre conventions, and of the concepts embedded in the overarching inquiry question guiding the study.

Nobis and his colleague Rick Cook were facing this set of challenges as they considered their students' need to create research papers. Nobis and Cook were bored with the uninspired and predictable topics and papers students had been composing for them over the years. Nobis describes the situation this way:

Rick and I both taught senior composition, i.e., "how to write a college academic essay." We were tired of the usual approach to the research paper, which usually looks something like this: "Pick a debatable social topic, conduct research, and write an essay using the research info as support. Cite sources using MLA documentation." If the teacher allows the student to choose his or her own topics, over 50% of the essays will be about abortion or legalizing marijuana, and almost every single one of them will be a stinkier of an essay. If the teacher doesn't allow students to choose, then you have a breeding ground for even stinkier essays and/or rampant plagiarism. (Nobis, personal communication, 2012)

Nobis and Cook decided to incorporate visual literacy in the early stages of the writing process by having their students read *Missouri Boy*, a graphic memoir by Leland Myrick. When they read with their students, Nobis and Cook focused on Myrick's choices of iconography and on the way Myrick framed the story within the panels of the story. They were informed by the sequencing principle that teaching proceeds from that which is close to students' experience to that which is further away, and from the visual and concrete to the nonvisual and abstract (see Smith and Wilhelm 2007). After students created their own graphic memoirs, Nobis and Cook asked students to pick a detail from their own comics (or from Myrick's if something in his scene really captured a student's interest) as a launching point for a research paper, which meant that students could pursue a wide range of topics or issues that came from their own experiences and interests—from their own story. Nobis describes one success story from his student Sam:

> Sam made his comic memoir about a time when he broke his foot. He was a little kid killing time while waiting for dinner to be served, saw a commercial on TV of a man dancing, and decided to dance too. His dance ended with an awkward twist, and he broke a foot. Early in the comic Sam included a panel of the kitchen in the background with a steak on a plate. In sharing his comic with a small peer group, he mentioned something about the steak in passing. Later on, Sam realized he had a question about the steak, completely unrelated to the plot of his memoir. Long story short, Sam researched the meat industry and how his steak ended up on his dinner plate, and ultimately wrote a paper about how beef, if grass fed and eaten in moderation, is good for you and not damaging to the planet as is sometimes reported. I like to think that without the graphic memoir miniunit first, he would've chosen a cliché topic and just gone through the motions instead of being invested and genuinely interested in his topic. (Nobis, personal communication, 2012)

This anecdote drives home the power of having students work with stories in both images and words. More precisely, when students are invited to investigate and write in both words and images, they can literally see things that they might have missed had they not worked in both. Which leads us to a second point:

Nobis let his students talk to one another about how they made decisions about what they included in their graphic memoirs. It was only after Sam was reading his work and talking with others about his choices that he discovered he had unanswered questions or curiosities about his experience.

Of course, not all students will have Sam's success. Some students, like the one mentioned previously, will resist. They will expect to do "school" writing. But as Nobis and Katie Wood Ray suggest, when students compose narratives using both words and images, when students examine and speculate about the choices other writers use when composing with words and images, then students have accessible concrete opportunities to understand narrative principles and to understand themselves as writers.

If we look at our narrative principles based on Bruner's description of the features of narrative, we can see how narratives using words and images can help students better understand those narrative principles (or, rather, how they might understand those principles in a way that only composing narratives with words might not afford).

Narrative Principles Based on Bruner's Features of Narrative	How Narratives Using Words and Images Might Help Students Develop Understanding of This Feature
A story shapes time.	Writers guide readers "through and between panels on a page or screen" (McCloud 2006, 10). Images and words can be used to show movement in time and over time.
A story focuses on particular events.	Writers must choose which moments to include in a piece and which to leave out, and writers choose which distance and angles readers can view those events. Authors of comics and graphic novels must carefully choose a few selected scenes, details, and events to imply a whole story.
A story shows changes in characters, especially in a character's values.	Writers choose how to render characters through the images and through the choice of words and the choice of how to arrange those words. Images can imply values and changes in values with a few salient details.
A story leads to interpretation by not always being explicit about what it means.	Writers make decisions about what to make visible and what to keep invisible, which means that readers are central to the meaning making of the text. Artists use the "whole world of visual iconography" (McCloud 1993, 202), which means that the meaning-making process relies on images, words, and how the reader and writer each understand the connection between the two. Comics have "gutters" between panels, which are inference gaps. Even photographs imply a pre- and post-text to the photograph.

(continues)

Narrative Principles Based on Bruner's Features of Narrative	How Narratives Using Words and Images Might Help Students Develop Understanding of This Feature
A story highlights a break in what was supposed to be or what was expected to be.	Images and words can help readers visualize what some of the expectations and breaks might look like.
A story creates a world with its own rules that must be adhered to within the story.	Writers choose how to represent the world in which the characters appear and interact. Some of that representation must be through the use of imagery.
A story is familiar and understandable in form.	Discussions on the features of form of visual media can be concrete and explicit (e.g., pointing to the panels in comics or a triptych, remarking on the speech bubbles, commenting on the size and shape of letters, etc.).
A story invites questions rather than posing solutions.	Writers use images to convey meaning (both textual descriptions and illustrations) to invite readers' interpretations.
A story builds on and is connected to other stories.	Texts can be periodical or serial, such as comic books, which build on one another and speak to each other. All formats often include details and references to other kinds of texts or events.

While Nobis and Cook focused on graphic memoirs, there are, of course, a wide range of narrative texts that use words and images, including other kinds of graphica (e.g., manga, comic strips, graphic novels, etc.), digital stories, video games, and picture books. We provide some key ideas about each of these kinds of stories; however, it's beyond the scope of this book to do each of these kinds of narratives justice. We do think, however, that the general principles of narratives can be learned and taught through any medium that use both words and images. The obvious distinctions between them would be the ways in which writers shape their stories into forms that are recognizable as graphica, digital stories, video games, or picture books.

The sequence that follows focuses on students creating picture books, but the same ideas and activities could be adapted for other kinds of narrative texts that use both words and images because they develop seminal tools of visual composing and visual literacy.

Composing to Plan

Framing instruction with an essential question helps students read purposefully and begin planning for their own composing throughout the unit. Asking such a question provides a purposeful context of use. The unit we describe here focuses on the essential question: "To what principles do people owe their primary allegiance?"

As teachers, we know that this idea of having to face competing principles at various moments is a very real and everyday occurrence. Lampert (1985) calls these moments "dilemmas," which she describes as "an argument between opposing tendencies within oneself in which neither side can come out the winner" (182). In teaching, for example, this might play out when we want to provide students with more feedback to all the texts they are creating, but we also want to have time to do other parts of our work (e.g., plan, confer, converse with colleagues, read professional literature, etc.) or to do things that matter in our lives (e.g., spend time with family, exercise, pursue hobbies, sleep, etc.). In other words, we are often faced with occasions when we must navigate a host of principles/values that we believe in (e.g., "extensive student feedback during the in-process stages of writing is helpful for students" in tension with "it's important to have some semblance of balance in our lives so as not to let our work consume all our free time"). This navigation of competing principles means that we have moments when it seems we have to make a choice. As Lampert would argue, it's not so much that we have either/or choices but that we need to focus "on the deliberation of one's alternatives rather than on a choice between them" (182). That is, it's not so much that we need to find panaceas that help to eliminate dilemmas, but that we find ways to read these moments and to respond in ways that move us forward.

With this idea that dilemmas are moments when people are faced with competing principles at play, we ask our students in this sequence to create a picture book (i.e., a narrative using words and images) to render the experience one character faces. We want the students to create characters who respond to a dilemma that places two or more principles/values in tension with one another or that places values in tension with an important goal. Having the students share their picture book with a reading buddy from an elementary school provided a real audience for the students and added gravitas and accountability to the project. Many students then worked with their reading buddies to help them write their own picture book.

> ➤ *Lesson idea*

The reading buddies provided a context that made the project matter. But to give students an even deeper sense of purpose, we suggest asking them to employ their interviewing skills (see Chapter 6) to talk with people of their own and older generations about dilemmas they have faced. Sharing the results of these interviews, first in small groups and then in whole-class discussions, helps students identify stories that they know would be important to tell.

As we begin to plan, we consider the inquiry square, because it helps us to name what we want our students to understand (about composing, about the specific kind of text and conventions of the genre they are creating, about the key concepts) and to do (as composers). For this sequence, our inquiry square looks like the following:

	Declarative Knowledge	Procedural Knowledge
Form	Understanding the features of a piece and how they are related to one another to create patterns that express meaning and create effects *Naming how the words and images work together to render this character's experience with a dilemma*	Knowing how to create the features of a piece and put them in relationship to each other in ways that help a reader recognize the genre and the expectations placed on the reader/interpreter, and the ways in which meaning and effect are expressed *Shaping the piece into a picture book (using a dialectic of words and images to help the reader notice what the composer wants the reader to notice); creating and ordering a series of images that reveal character, setting, an intensifying dilemma, reactions and responses and that work with words to tell a story of conflicted loyalty that comes to a clear resolution* *For images, students producing illustrations that use details revealing more about the character/ storyworld setting/action, or the passage of time than what is in the words; to make decisions about using more or less detail than the words; to use images to abet or contradict the words (often for humor); to position the images and words in relation to one another; to use different kinds of images to do different kinds of work for expressing meaning and creating effect*
Substance	Understanding the concepts within a piece and how those concepts work together *Naming what the character reveals about what people should be most loyal to . . . and how this is expressed through the specific details, images, and overall patterning and construction of the text*	Knowing how to go about gaining conceptual understanding and generating story elements in word and image that express meaning and create significant effects that abet that meaning *Creating characters, time, storyworld, dilemmas, conflict and consequences, filters/slant that reveal a character faced with a dilemma of principles*

Composing to Practice

As we begin the instructional sequence, we read mentor texts, first using picture books, noting what we think is important. We choose classic picture books that deal with principles, dilemmas, and conflicted loyalty, like the Holocaust tale *Rose Blanche* (Innocento), or the story of conflicting views of learning expressed by *John Patrick Norman McHennesy Goes to School* (Burningham).

➤ *Lesson idea*

With that preparation, the class can use the Frayer model to figure out what we think of *loyalty* and *principles*.

➤ *Lesson idea*

Examples of LOYALTY	Traits of LOYALTY, or Traits Associated with LOYALTY
"Near" examples of LOYALTY (what looks or sounds like loyalty, but isn't quite loyalty?) and nonexamples	Define LOYALTY

Examples of PRINCIPLES	Qualities/ Traits of PRINCIPLES or Principled People, or Principled Action, or Associations
"Near" examples of PRINCIPLES (what looks or sounds like a principle, but isn't quite a principle?) or nonexamples	Define PRINCIPLE/ PRINCIPLED

And then we ask students, "How do people stay loyal to their principles?" and "How and why might one's sense of loyalty or principles change?" At this stage, we are trying to get our students to write and to share what they think about these key concepts of loyalty and principles. This move also provides an opportunity for autobiographical writing about real experiences where someone dealt with conflicted loyalties.

Next, we have students rank a range of principles in their order of importance using the following activity:

PRINCIPLES RANKING

Directions: Rank each of these principles in order of importance to you: 1 is most important; 25 is least important. Avoid ties.

_____ Achievement (good grades, athletic success, etc.)	_____ Love
	_____ Friendship
_____ Power/influence	_____ Family
_____ Fitting in	_____ Excitement/stimulation
_____ Generosity	_____ Health
_____ Hope	_____ Honesty
_____ Altruism/sacrifice	_____ Curiosity
_____ Pleasing parents and authorities	_____ Peace of mind
_____ Enjoyment	_____ Money
_____ Faith	_____ Artistry/artistic expression
_____ Patriotism	_____ Environmentalism
_____ Compassion	_____ Security
_____ Competitiveness	_____ ???

After you rank the items, write for a few minutes about the decisions that were most difficult for you and why those were hard decisions.

After you write about how you made your decisions, share with at least two other people about your choices and their choices. Be prepared to talk about any patterns you notice with all the choices you heard about or to talk about any choices that stuck out to you.

➤ *CCSS reading for main idea, attention to author decisions*

We like to have students do a ranking first for themselves since that is closest to home. Then we ask them to do it for some of the characters they've been reading about in the mentor texts, showing how values stayed the same or evolved throughout a book. Finally, we have students use the ranking to plan their own book, asking what will confirm and reinforce values, what will change and transform values, and what theme is expressed by these processes.

After ranking personal principles, we take a look at the *principle continuum* (or what we sometimes refer to as the "principle tug-of-war." This activity is based on McKee's (1997) "value changes" and on Egri's (1960) "unity of opposites." This kind of practice is essential because in stories the thematic meaning is always wrapped up with character change and why and how the characters change for the worse or better.

➤ *Lesson idea*

Directions: On this set of continua, you will see a range within a principle. We'll start by marking where a character we're all familiar with from films or TV seems to fall. Then you'll do this for yourself: How would you rate where you are on these continua when you are in a good mood? How about when you are frustrated or challenged by an intense situation or conflict? How about when you were younger versus now? How about when you are older and leading younger people?

Finally, you will mark where you think a character you've been reading about, know well, or are creating for your story falls within each principle at the beginning of a story/when you first met, then in a unique situation, and then how they may have developed and changed over time. Consider what might explain any changes in values that you can discern so you can share these insights with a thinking partner.

(Character's Name) _____

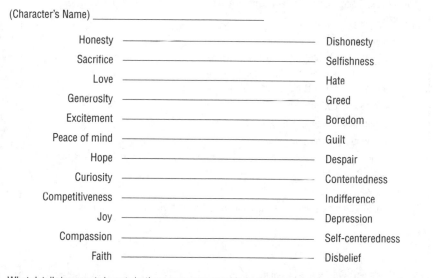

Honesty	Dishonesty
Sacrifice	Selfishness
Love	Hate
Generoslty	Greed
Excitement	Boredom
Peace of mind	Guilt
Hope	Despair
Curiosity	Contentedness
Competitiveness	Indifference
Joy	Depression
Compassion	Self-centeredness
Faith	Disbelief

What details/moments/events/actions were you considering as you placed a character on each continuum? How were the marks similar or different at the beginning of the story compared to the struggle the character faced in the middle of the story compared to where the character seemed to be at the end of the story? Which values stayed firm and which moved?

Students place marks on the continua, then write in response to the questions we ask, then share with partners, then debrief as a whole class. At the end of the whole-class conversation, students are asked to write briefly on this prompt: "What have you noticed today about what causes people to change values and principles? What are the kinds of moments that challenge people to stay loyal to their principles? What causes people to go back and forth during their own principle tug-of-war?"

At this point, we have had students think quite a bit about principles and how people navigate their principles. They've developed the declarative knowledge they need to write. It's here when we want to help students begin to develop the procedural knowledge that they need to think about dramatizing dilemmas through characters, so we begin to help them create characters who are faced with competing principles by generating possible specific moments that create dilemmas.

➤ *Lesson idea*

We've used the following assignment to help us do so.

Directions: Sketch out characters, setting, and a specific conflict involving some of the following:

- a punishment—fair or unfair
- a choice that is difficult—whether to dance with someone you don't like or to ask someone to dance who you like but who has a steady, being asked on a date while your steady is out of town
- lies and deceptions
- accusations—true or somewhat true or false
- encounter with rival or authority
- parent finds something you have hidden from them, like a spare key to the car, or letter from school
- answering the phone while playing hooky
- being with a person or in a situation that endangers you, like with a driver who is drinking
- an accident
- an impulsive action
- trying to avoid a responsibility
- giving something up
- an embarrassment
- an unexpected arrival.

After students have sketched out some ideas, we ask them to stretch the conflict and intensify the consequences:

- Intensify an idea, character value, character trait, timeline, element of the situation, immediacy of the problem that will magnify the situation and consequences.

- Change the beginning, ending, or the color, setting, object, shape, motion, size, or sound of something.

- Add another character, value, action, weather, prop, and so on.

- Make something more or less accurate, predictable, important, important, readable, emotional.

- Make something more or less important: value, person, sign, and so on.

- Rearrange or reverse the situation: parent is caught by kids hiding something from them.

Another way to use this activity is for students to work in small groups sharing their ideas and creatively combining situations, characters, and ideas to see if interesting new combinations come up that explore a conflict in values and loyalties that they might want to write about. This helps students consider unexpected conflicts and get outside the box of their own experience.

After creating a number of situations that involve dilemmas, as well as a number of characters who might face these dilemmas, students share with one another. First they share with partners, then small groups, and then they post what they consider to be the five best ideas for dilemmas and characters on chart paper around the room. As students are sharing and posting, they search for characters and dilemmas that they are drawn to. Once they have three characters and three dilemmas, then students take note cards and draw a quick sketch of the character on one side and the dilemma on the other side. We ask them to consider how the dilemma involves values and how each conflict leads to high stakes and different consequences. We ask students to do this for a few characters (maybe three) so that they have multiple characters to work with, and especially for those moments when they may feel stuck or when they may lose interest in a character or story that heads in a dead-end direction for them. Multiple possibilities can help alleviate some of the pressure if that kind of moment occurs in the creative pro-cess—as it certainly will for some students.

Early Draft Composing

After students have some characters and dilemmas to work with, we begin *sketching out possible storylines*. We use a series of boxes to help students begin to visualize the elements of their stories.

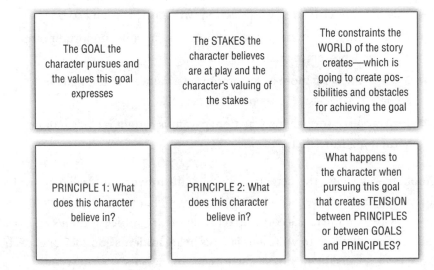

The GOAL the character pursues and the values this goal expresses

The STAKES the character believes are at play and the character's valuing of the stakes

The constraints the WORLD of the story creates—which is going to create possibilities and obstacles for achieving the goal

PRINCIPLE 1: What does this character believe in?

PRINCIPLE 2: What does this character believe in?

What happens to the character when pursuing this goal that creates TENSION between PRINCIPLES or between GOALS and PRINCIPLES?

Once students seem to have a solid idea of the parts of their story, then we begin to work with the skeleton of the story. The structure of this kind of story can be fairly simple because of the target audience (young readers) and genre (picture book): a character faces a complication and then engages in a struggle before the complication is resolved. One important thing to note about the strug-gle is that we want students to make sure the character first takes action toward his or her goal before she or he offers a reaction to an ensuing complication or before another, competing goal is introduced. This matters, particularly at the sentence level (it's one way to help students think about the order of informa-tion presented to a reader within a sentence). The action–reaction pattern also works at a broader text level, and it helps students structure what might happen within the section of the story that focuses on a character's struggle in pursuing his or her goal. In the graphic that follows, we note that the series of actions–reactions would be a way to structure the struggle a character faces in resolving the complication (and there can be fewer or more action–reaction pairs in the chain). In our story, the complication might simply be the competing principles or might be some outer goal that complicates the inner life of the character (the competing principles or tension between principles and goals); it depends on how sophisticated you want your students to be in their storylines.

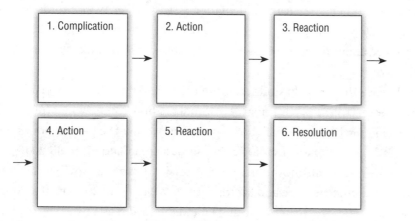

Finally, we ask students to create storyboards for the picture book. This is when students begin to consider the actual pages of the book, which means they will begin to figure out where the words and images will appear on specific pages. Depending on how long your students' books are, you might consider creating a graphic that students can use to sketch ideas on the pages. It might look like this:

Page 1	Page 2

Page 3	Page 4

And so on. Picture books for people ages three to eight use relatively few words and typically have twenty-four to thirty-two pages (Lamb 2001). For our students, we might cut that by half (twelve to sixteen pages), depending on their needs and desires as writers. Writers do need enough space to show a character struggling with a situation in which two principles are at odds or are in tension with one another, so that might lengthen a story in terms of words or in terms of pages. Once students have begun to storyboard, then we might return to what we noticed about the features of a picture book when we looked at models earlier in the sequence.

Now it's time to help students move their idea from the storyboard and from conversations to the paper (or screen). Students find it hugely helpful to focus on composing the beginnings of stories, so we like to use the picture books we have been reading as mentor texts for doing so (Dorfman and Cappelli 2007). Whenever we help students move their writing forward, we are moving the *writer* forward for the current piece and for the future. We tell our students that Stephanie Harvey describes the writer as an angler and the reader as a fish. The beginning is the bait to hook the reader, and we have a range of options for baiting our hook.

One move that we highlight is creating a what-if scenario. In *Elizabeth Leads the Way: Elizabeth Cady Stanton and the Right to Vote* (2008) by Tanya Lee Stone, the book begins

> What would you do
> if someone told you
> you can't be what you want to be
> because you are a girl?
>
> What would you do
> if someone told you
> your vote doesn't count,
> your voice doesn't matter
> because you are a girl?
>
> Would you ask why?
> Would you talk back?
> Would you fight . . .
> for your rights?
>
> Elizabeth did. (1)

After rereading and discussing this beginning, we write a model beginning based on it. Then students write beginnings for their own stories based on this model, directly asking the reader about how they would respond to a dilemma involving values that are analogous to those in the story. We look at the pictures accompanying the beginning of the Cady book, and then brainstorm the kinds of pictures we could use with our beginnings and how they would work with the words to create an engaging and informative beginning, leading to a dilemma of values.

Another move we highlighted is sharing a secret that is surprising and adds an unexpected value or principle into the mix from the very beginning. For example in *George Washington and the General's Dog*, Frank Murphy (2002) tells the story of how George Washington called a truce to return the British General Howe's dog after this valued pet followed the Revolutionary Army home after a battle. The story opens: "George Washington is one of America's greatest heroes. Most people know that George was honest and brave. But there is something about George that people don't always know. George Washington *loved* animals" (5-6). Since this love of animals caused a conflict with other values, like winning independence, this secret leads directly to a dilemma in values. Again, students read and discuss the mentor text. We write a beginning for a story that follows this model, then students work in pairs or alone to compose their own beginnings.

Another move is to create a sense of era. If our students are writing about a character from another era, or about a dilemma that stretches into the past, this is a great move. In Kathleen Krull's *Wilma Unlimited: How Wilma Rudolph Became Wilma Rudolph*, the story begins:

> No one expected such a tiny girl to have a first birthday. In Clarksville, Tennessee, in 1940, life for a baby who weighed just over four pounds at birth was sure to be limited.
>
> But most babies didn't have nineteen older brothers and sisters to watch over them. Most babies didn't have a mother who knew home remedies and a father who worked several jobs.
>
> Most babies weren't Wilma Rudolph. (1996, 1)

We ask students what makes an era, and how they could portray this in images and in words. What makes today: the President (Obama), technology (iPhones, Nooks), historical events (Arab Spring), popular movies (*Puss in Boots*), clothing styles, popular music and musical groups (Katy Perry, Adele, etc.). What makes yesterday, like the sixties?

Next we focus on endings, reminding students that Ralph Fletcher tells us that the ending is the part that will echo in the ear of the reader, that the ending is the kick into the finish line, the part that is most important to the meaning and effect of the story. Again, we choose endings of our favorite picture books and use them as mentor texts—we study the model, then the teacher creates an ending following that model with student feedback and help, then students work in pairs and alone to create endings following the model.

We also want students to focus on three key moves writers and illustrators make during their stories: the use of repetition (in words and in images), the use of parallelism (in words and in images), and the placement of words and images in power positions. We ask students to share with a few other people, focusing on one of these at a time. The idea here isn't for students to have it all figured out; instead, it's to help them see options and to provide one another with possible choices they might make in the images, in the words, or in the way the words and images work with one another. This leads us into drafting.

Repetition for images and words are signals to readers that something is important. This repetition might be icons, names, numbers, beginnings/endings of phrases, key words, movements, expressions, colors, and so on. An image might be repeated by change in some way through the story in a manner that reinforces meaning or effect. Just like with teaching beginnings and endings, we use mentor texts (mentor sentences or mentor pages from the texts we have read) as models to follow as we practice noticing repetitions of words and/or images. We use the classic children's book *Madeline* by Bemelmans to show how phrases and pictures are repeated, subtly changed, and contrasted to move a story forward and create meanings and effects.

Parallelism for words and images are signals to readers that something is important. This parallelism might be the patterns of beginning or ending sentences, might be the use of opposites (like in images—e.g., a hot one, a cold one; a tall one, a short one, etc.). We use the beginning of *Bats! Strange and Wonderful* by Laurence Pringle (2000) where he engages in extended repetitions using parallel structure: "If you were a bat, you could stay awake all night long" (1) and he repeats the structure and phrase "If you were a bat, you could . . ." throughout the book. The repetition and parallelism help young readers remember and feel a rhythm to the story. It sets up patterns that can then be broken to help the reader notice something that might be important.

Power positions (or privileged positions, if you prefer) for words are largely at the ends of units (end of a sentence, end of a section, end of the entire thing) because that's what readers are left to remember. Power positions for images might be top/bottom of pages; right-hand side of pages (since that's the page readers turn from), use of colors that stand in contrast to others, and so on. We ask students to study a picture book of their own choosing and share in small groups how the author helped his or her young readers recognize what's most important to attend to.

Final Draft Composing

Once students have created a rough draft, we want them to step back from the storytelling and picture book–making process, to think about their experience. We ask them to do the following: "Tell the story of *how* you wrote what you wrote. What were some difficult decisions or obstacles you faced and how did you handle them?" We ask students to write for several minutes about their experiences, and then we ask them to meet with others to share the choices that were difficult. Then, we ask students to write on the board (or on chart paper) the most difficult challenge they are facing as writers of picture books. Once everyone has posted one challenge, then we attempt to categorize them. Once we have categories, we write about and talk about possibilities in handling those challenges. (This obviously also constitutes a kind of composing to transfer, because students are reflecting on their experiences learning and writing and how to bring this learning forward into the future.)

Next, we want to spend some time for students to create covers for their picture books. We think the covers of such texts should both be appealing to the audience and capture and introduce the big principles (or theme) that compete with one another in the story. We think about the colors used, the kind and style of lettering, the placement of images and words, and so on. This work on the covers begins to move students toward synthesizing what they see happening in their stories and how it starts to address the larger question, "What should people most be loyal to?"

We like to pick out one or two issues for proofreading. One issue that often comes up is the use of apostrophes and possessive pronouns because a character is going to own values and principles. We admire Jeff Anderson's (2007) work in *Everyday Editing* where he provides some models of correct usage, for example:

Alan Ferko's face turned red as Bo Peep's pigtail ribbons.

—**Jerry Spinelli**, *Stargirl* (2000, 9)

We like to provide three such examples, often using the students' own writing, then ask students what they notice and have them create a rule and proofreading cue for apostrophes for possession. We can then move to plural possessives and possessive pronouns.

You can combine work on proofreading for correct apostrophe use, or for possessive pronouns, and differentiating *it's* (it is), *its* (possessive pronoun) and *its'* (which does not exist!) while reviewing specific showing writing. Anderson does this by providing a boring "telling" rewrite of some vivid professional descriptive writing and then comparing the versions, for example:

I don't like her Christmas tree at all.

versus

Don't even get me started about my Aunt Rose's Christmas tree. First of all, it's aluminum. Second of all, it's pink. I mean, like the color of Pepto-Bismol, which makes sense, because I get sick to my stomach just looking at it.

—**Neal Shusterman**,
The Schwa Was Here (2006) (Anderson 2007, 81)

We have students compare and discuss the two examples, review the use of *it's*, and then proofread and revise their own papers on the basis of our discussion. Of course, multiple examples can give the students the requisite practice.

Composing to Transfer

At the end of this sequence, we want students to reflect on how they thought their characters faced dilemmas. We might ask the following questions: What principle seems to be most important to your character? How is this like or unlike situations you or someone you know has faced? What surprised you about how the character faced the dilemma? In what way is this character like you and in what way is this character different than you? How does this character represent what you think is important (or not) for young people to know about facing dilemmas?

Finally, we want to give our students a chance to read one another's finished picture books. We have students return to the principle tug-of-war by having them pay attention to how characters in other books composed by classmates struggled with one or more principles. Then students read their stories to their reading buddies, and many of our students play the tug-of-war with their buddies.

This helps our students note how a wide range of characters the class created responded to dilemmas. We ask students: What patterns do you see in how our characters responded to dilemmas? What outliers do you notice? What is absent? What do we seem to believe as a class about what people should most be loyal to? What might someone else say to challenge what seems to be our collective belief?

Transfer to Digital Stories

Of course, picture books are not the only kind of narrative that employs both words and images; however, they do focus on how things work or on how problems are solved, which means that they are suited for a wide range of disciplinary conversations. As a follow-up to the reading buddy picture book project where our students write picture books for their buddies, in the next semester our students write digital stories both *for* and then *with* their reading buddies to explore the inquiry "What makes a good community?"

The Center for Digital Storytelling (2011) defines "digital story" as "a short, first person video-narrative created by combining recorded voice, still and moving images, and music or other sounds." The power of digital stories, according to Leslie Rule of the Digital Storytelling Association, come from a writer "weaving images, music, narrative, and voice together, thereby giving deep dimension and vivid color to characters" (Barrett 2004).

We've found many benefits of digital storytelling. Foremost among them is the holding power of technology. Particularly for our resistant and struggling writers, digital storytelling is engaging and compelling and a great way for them to experiment with and develop their voice. We've also found that digital storytelling, being in the first person, helps our students identify as writers, and—because these stories are so easily shared—to build community. That made digital storytelling doubly effective for our inquiry into what makes a good community. One of the ways is obviously to share and be respectful of one another's stories, in this case stories of community, of being outsiders or of fitting in, a powerful move for social action and transformation (see Chapter 9).

In this project, we consolidated and further developed what the students knew about storytelling and about moviemaking. We were able to make connections between the visual conventions of movies and the textual conventions of more traditional stories (like using setting to create mood and set invitations and constraints to characters in that setting). Our students, and then their reading buddies, create three- to five-minute digital stories using iMovies, but other teachers we know have used the latest versions of PhotoStory.

When creating digital stories and movies, writers render an experience though the filter of a character from among a variety of choices in both the words presented in a script and the images presented on the screen. These choices include not only storyboarding the images and drafting a script (typically two hundred to three hundred words) to overplay the images seen on the screen, but also the ethical decisions of fair use for images and audio used to tell a story—an important thing to know in our digital world, and a useful way to teach students how to avoid plagiarism.

➤ *CCSS connection*

In the planning and practicing phases of this project, we work with students to identify fair use standards and apply these. We also spend considerable time helping students select images that go with their story, and that express character, setting, perspective, and other story features highlighted in the Common Core State Standards (CCSS). We likewise practice selecting music that expresses mood and psychological feeling and that complements various moments in the story. This is a great chance to introduce students to great artwork and various kinds of music. We also explore different ways of using titles, captions, and transitions between scenes and compare these visual navigational devices to transitions in written texts.

We ask: What do you want your audience to know and to experience? What do you want your audience to have to figure out, and how will you help them figure this out? How will the images and sounds help them experience the story in the way you want?

We use the same criteria as we did for the picture book, but add sound and music to the criteria about images. Students share stories at a reading buddy extravaganza and also at a friends and family after-school gathering, providing students with multiple audiences for their work.

Other possibilities for transfer abound. Much of the work students did in writing their picture books and in composing the digital stories is also relevant to graphica. Terry Thompson (2008) defines *graphica* as "a medium of literature that integrates pictures and words and arranges them cumulatively to tell a story or convey information" (6). He then divides graphica into different formats, including comic strips, comic books, graphic novels, and manga. Within each of these formats, writers can write about real or imagined events or experiences, including but not limited to realistic fiction, biography, historical fiction, memoir, romance, true crime, adventure stories, human interest stories, and much, much more. Thus, the substance of graphica, like any kind of story, includes characters, time, storyworlds, and filters and slants; however, unlike other kind of stories, the features of graphica mean that writers have particular kind of choices to represent that substance.

- Panels, frames, and gutters (the spaces between panels) show the passage of time, a sense of the storyworld, and the perspective and focus the writer wants the reader to follow.
- Speech and thought bubbles capture what character say to one another (speech bubbles) or to oneself (thought bubbles), which in turn, helps the reader infer the mood of the situation.
- Exposition boxes (often near the top or bottom of a panel) establish or reestablish any of the narrative threads such as time and place.
- Lettering (the shape of words) creates mood or assists readers with intonation or phrasing.
- Directionality (the arrangement of text and images) guides a reader's focus. (Thompson 2008)

Of course, comic strips and books, graphic novels, and manga do have some differences between one another. Thompson (2008) notes the following distinctions:

- Comic strips are typically three to eight panels—think the kind of comics you might find in the newspaper or, increasingly, online.
- Comic books are periodical and the story continues from issue to issue.
- Graphic novels are of book length and the story line typically starts and ends within the same text.
- Manga are Japanese-style graphic novels that include stylized drawings, simplified features, and outlines and are often read from back to front.

Our suggestion of how to teach graphica is consistent with the approach we suggested for storybooks:

- Have students investigate and discuss the work such texts do in the world and create a context that resembles as nearly as possible those real-world conditions.
- Help students understand the elements of the kind of text they plan to create through the examination of mentor texts.
- Give students practice in producing those elements, especially those that are unique (e.g., speech bubbles).
- Have students draft their texts and then revise them based on the feedback of their colleagues.
- Create an occasion for meaningfully sharing the results of their labors.

Perhaps the most sophisticated kind of narrative is the interactive narrative, which often employs words and images. "Interactive narrative is a time-based representation of character and action in which a reader can affect, choose, or change the plot. The first-, second-, or third-person character may actually be the reader" (Meadows 2003, 62). Opinion and perspective are inherent. Video games are the most interactive of narratives, because they position players into the role of making decisions that affect the plot of the story. Because of this choice players have, composers of video games make structural decisions to create multiple filters players can follow during the course of the story.

In interactive narratives, like video games, the reader and the text have a bidirectional relationship that is visible in that the reader shapes the text and the text shapes the reader. The writer is charged with making those moments possible and logical. The video game, like other interactive narratives, is a demanding kind of narrative that can employ both words and images. Because many young people are familiar with video games, we think it can be a useful, though challenging, kind of narrative to analyze and to create.

We understand that working with words and images may seem to some to be frivolous, given the deserved attention that composing more conventionally academic texts get. But we think that there's time for both. In fact, we think it's crucial to make that time. Being literate has always meant the capacity to compose and receive meanings with a culture's most powerful tools (Bolter 2001; Wilhelm, Friedemann, and Erickson 1998). Those tools are now digital and multimodal and use visuals. Unless students are taught to be critical readers, composers, and users of digital multimodal literacies, they can hardly be said to be literate.

CHAPTER 9

How Narrative Can Serve Young People

*I wanted a perfect ending. Now I've learned, the hard way, that
some poems don't rhyme, and some stories don't have a clear beginning,
middle, and end. Life is about not knowing, having to change,
taking the moment and making the best of it, without knowing what's
going to happen next. Delicious Ambiguity.*

—Gilda Radner

Our work in this book is based on a profound belief that reading and writing narratives can foster new understandings of oneself and others, understandings that empower people to do real and important work in the world. We hope that we've convinced you of the power of narrative and have shown you some ways that you can help your students experience that power. And we hope that we've established that the Common Core State Standards (CCSS) can be useful guides in that effort.

But we realize that the CCSS and the assessments that are being developed to measure them place more emphasis on argument and exposition than they do on narrative in the upper grades, so we worry a bit that the writing of narratives will be underemphasized as teachers and schools respond to these assessments. In our minds, that would be a huge mistake.

The CCSS are designed to ensure that all students are prepared for college and for the world of work. As we argued in our initial chapters, it's impossible to provide that preparation without significant attention to the unique and powerful way of knowing narrative provides. The *Routledge Encyclopedia of Narrative Theory* (2005) provides a succinct summary of our argument: "The past several decades have seen an explosion of interest in narrative, with this multifaceted object of inquiry becoming a central concern in a wide range of disciplinary fields and research contexts."

In and of itself, then, narrative is crucially important for personal, interpersonal, educational, and professional growth. But, at the risk of sounding like infomercial salesmen, that's not all. It also provides the vehicle to help students develop other understandings highlighted by the CCSS.

Fulford (2000) writes that "stories demand ethical understanding. There's no such thing as *just* a story. A story is always charged with meaning; otherwise it is not a story, merely a sequence of events" (6). As we've argued elsewhere (Smith and Wilhelm 2010), the five kinds of knowledge that we build this book around are just as important for readers as they are for writers. Both need to understand why they are doing what they are doing and how the immediate and wider context affects what they can and are expected to do. Writers need to know how to get the stuff about which they will write; readers need to draw on their prior knowledge and recognize how to mine texts for what they want to learn from them. Writers need to be able to create the formal features of the texts they are trying to produce; readers need to recognize these formal features and enact the reading conventions they invite.

Let's look at the some of CCSS anchor standards for reading for a more specific illustration. Standard 2 calls for students to "determine central ideas or themes of a text and analyze their development; summarize the key supporting details and ideas." How better to know what details are important than to include them in one's own writing. Standard 3 calls on students to "analyze how and why individuals, events, and ideas develop and interact over the course of a text." Think of all of the work we've suggested on developing scenes and how that work would pay off for students' subsequent reading. Standard 6 calls for students to "assess how point of view or purpose shapes the content and style of a text." Think of all of our work with filters and slants and how by creating characters with different perspectives our students might ask questions about how other writers have crafted the filters and slants they use in the texts they created.

We could go on, but we think our point is clear: If we want our students to be better readers, we need to help them become competent and aware writers. But yet again, that's not all. Narrative complements and even directly serves the other kinds of writing the CCSS call for. Think of how many public policy arguments depend on narratives. Calls for universal health care, marriage equality, extending unemployment benefits are almost always made by spinning out the stories of those who are affected by such policies. Think of how extended definitions of abstract concepts depend both on illustrative narrative and counternarratives. And still more. Look at CCSS writing anchor standard 7:

➤ Writing anchor standard 7

> Conduct short as well as more sustained research projects to answer a question (including a self-generated question) or solve a problem; narrow or broaden the inquiry when appropriate; synthesize multiple sources on the subject, demonstrating understanding of the subject under investigation.

Narrative as a Mode of Inquiry

Schaafsma, Vinz, and the National Conference on Research in Language and Literacy (2011) explain why narrative inquiry would be such a powerful way to achieve this standard. They write that narrative:

1. Makes visible the puzzles of mind—framings, evidences, stances, theories, and questions—in the researcher's composing of the text
2. Challenges its own questions, answers, possibilities, and theories
3. Grapples with issues of responsibility, power, relations, and ethics as it evidences the importance of learning with others
4. Works to redefine the products or outcomes of research. (8)

Oftentimes, inquiry or research seems to focus on certainty, on sameness, rather than "dwell[ing] on differences to find elements that undermine certainty and generalizability" (Schaafsma, Vinz, and the National Conference on Research in Language and Literacy 2011, 25). In our own research, we've found that sameness is very rare. Narrative as a research tool will help students grapple with the messy complexity that they are sure to find in any question of interest.

We believe this is important for the young people and teachers with whom we work, because so much of what happens during one's learning or writing process is not certain and is highly dependent on a whole host of contextual and task-specific features. We want students to be able to notice, name, and share the story of their learning and of their writing. That's why in our "Composing to Transfer" sections of Chapters 5, 6, 7, and 8 we have students look back at their writing experiences, identifying patterns and gaps and obstacles. We want our students to inquire into their own stories as writers. To provide another example of what this might look like, we present Sarah Woodard, an eighth-grade teacher in Denver and a Co-Director of the Denver Writing Project.

➤ *CCSS connection*

In Sarah's classes students write often, and they do their writing in online spaces. All early drafts of their writing are done on Google Docs, where students and Sarah can make comments, ask questions, point out strong passages or moves, and more. The drafts and the revision history is archived for students. Once students are ready to share a more final version, they upload PDF files of their pieces on to their own personal Google Sites. Again, the site becomes a location for students to archive the wide range of texts they create: it's a portfolio.

➤ *CCSS on multimodal texts, use of technology, process of writing*

Yet, Sarah does not stop there with her students. Her aim isn't simply to have students finish a piece (although that is a challenge for some students), but rather to think about what they have learned as writers. In other words, she wants students to use narrative as a mode of inquiry into their own learning and writing process—as a kind of composing to transfer, in our terms. Sarah asks students to write reflections about their process in which they point out moments when they revised and why they made those choices. They point to comments or questions that moved them forward or that caused them to think in a new direction. Her students are making visible their thinking over time, raising questions and possibilities, and grappling with their next steps and future contexts. In other words, they are engaging in narrative inquiry, discovering and telling the story of their own process.

Narrative as an Object of Inquiry

Of course, narrative is not just a mode of inquiry, but narratives are also objects of inquiry as well. We make the argument that composing narratives is a helpful way for students to understand narrative principles and that applying those narrative principles in their lives can help students understand and potentially change the way they understand themselves, others, and the world. What do we do to help our students make this leap? We ask them to study how narratives work in the world, such as when we have them analyze the work individual stories and collections of stories do for people and communities.

For example, we looked at the Into/Through/Beyond framework (Rymes 2009), as an analytic for helping students better understand what happens when a storyteller shares one story with an audience. We want students to think about what initiates stories, how it positions individuals and groups represented within the story, and how the story and the storytelling exchange affect the people and groups after the story is shared. Students might listen to and analyze stories shared in their families, in the circle of friends, or really in any group they participate in. This kind of analysis is an invitation for students to understand what happens in their groups and the role that stories play within those communities. They can see people, including themselves, in a new way, and they might better understand how stories shape the relationships and the roles and the identities people take within those groups. They can then craft new stories—stories that make themselves, others, or their communities healthier or more empowered.

We also want students to think about how stories work together as collections. We presented Lee Ann Bell's (2010) framework. In this framework, stories are categorized by how they function within a community—stock stories, concealed stories, resistance stories, and emerging/transformative stories. Students are invited to understand the ways in which a collection of stories can become "common sense" and how they can be a way to challenge or change that "common sense." For instance, students might investigate stories about "girls" or "boys" or "teens" or "class" or "race" or any number of other social constructs. We think this kind of analytical work can help students both critique and change their world. Being able to see and understand how stories build on one another and how stories work together to shape the way people see themselves and others is a tool for participating in their communities. It's a participatory skill to be able to step back and understand how stories position and shape what happens in a community. It's a way to empower the young people in our classrooms.

We know that composing narratives can help students understand themselves, others, ideas, and their world. We know that composing narratives can deepen and develop students' understanding of narrative principles that will help them become better and more eager readers.

We also know that composing narratives can be a doorway toward possibility and change, toward transformation and justice, toward awareness and empowerment. Composing narratives can lead to hope. There is nothing that our own students seem to want more for themselves. There's nothing that our world needs more. It's worth working and teaching and storytelling for.

Appendix A

Photographs and Soundtracks

Jim Fredricksen

Throw away the lights, the definitions
And say of what you see in the dark

—Wallace Stevens

Mr. O'Conner, on old and lonely man, took a slow, deep swallow of water and sat in his tattered leather chair in his well-lit living room that was once filled with the smile of his wife and the energy of his son. His belly had the *Logan Daily Newspaper* spread across it, and the afternoon sun mixed with all of the lights he had on. He was a large and once jovial man with uncombed hair, white and thin, and the wrinkles and bags under his eyes made him look as tired as he felt. It was Friday afternoon, just after his bowl of potato soup and his hands, large enough to make the soup bowl disappear, quivered when he put the glass of water on the table between his chair and the couch. The first spring bird rested on the sill of his picture window and nothing in Northern Minnesota is as welcoming as the first warm day breaking the string of gray clouds and hazy overcast light.

Mr. O'Conner took a deep breath and the date on the paper made him realize that it was twenty-seven days since the funeral of his only son, Johnny, whose picture was on top of the television, on the walls, and mixed in with all the other black-and-white photos. All the photographs reminded Mr. O'Conner of his own father, an amateur photographer, who believed that the world was his own personal canvas for photographs. From the chair, Mr. O'Conner stared back at the eyes in all the photographs in the room, moving from Johnny to Louise to his own parents to his colleagues from the paper—all deceased or away in a home for the aged and broken.

He began to read the paper, filled with all the stories of people living life, suffering, joyful, connected. Mr. O'Conner breathed deeply again and he noticed that the light began to fade on Mrs. Hawkins's car across the street. The car, a beat-up blue Chevy Nova, reminded him of his father. "Michael," his father would say, "Light itself is always invisible. We see only things, only objects, not light."

Light was always so scientific to his father, but Mr. O'Conner remembered the orange and red sunset on Fox Lake in 1954 when Louise looked warm and young and she said, "Of course I'll marry you." He recalled the yellowish light making the other soon-to-be fathers look nervous as they didn't talk to one another in the waiting room. He remembers the moonlight on the street outside his home, the car lights shining on one another early in the winter mornings as he headed off to work, and the kerosene light glowing around Johnny when they'd go ice fishing. Light was always there and his father put it in his thoughts as a way to remember the important moments.

He started reading the paper again. When he got to the sports section, he read about his young neighbor, Amanda Hawkins, who was a seventeen-year-old basketball player for Logan High. From their record, the team wouldn't make the playoffs and tonight would be the last game for the three seniors, including Amanda. Even though it was her last game, Amanda couldn't play because of her knee injury. It had been four weeks since he had a visitor, and it had been nearly twenty-five years since he stepped foot in the high school, twenty-five years since Johnny was in high school. Mr. O'Conner knew he needed to leave the house, but he'd have to walk and it would take him nearly forty-five minutes to go the five blocks to the school.

He sat, not wanting to move. For the next hour, his water became warmer and the front yard grew darker and darker. The lights in the living room were fighting to take over from the daylight, and the muscles in his back began to ache. Why couldn't he get himself to move?

Louise stared back at him from her picture on the windowsill and above the couch that lined up in front of the window. Johnny had been the last one on the couch. He was only forty-three when he died. Skin cancer got the best of him after only six months from the diagnosis. He sat right there on that couch and said, "Pop, I don't want you to be scared, but I got cancer. Skin cancer." Johnny kept on talking, but at the time all Mr. O'Conner could think about was all the summer days when Johnny would mow lawn after lawn in the neighborhood. He thought about him playing ball on the asphalt courts with the sun beating down on him. He thought about Johnny playing golf, taking cruises, working on his tan. The sun damaged and then finally destroyed his son. What kind of legacy did he leave his Johnny?

Mr. O'Conner took a deep breath, his belly rising, and said to Louise, "I've got to go, don't I?" The silence reminded him that he only had pictures, only snapshots of when he felt connected, attached, complete. Now, he was broken and cut off. After he managed to get himself up, he put on a clean shirt and he threw on his Twins baseball cap. He heard himself whistling an old song he couldn't name and he realized he felt a slight twinge of excitement. "I'm going to a ball game," he said to Johnny before he turned off all the lights.

Logan High School was two blocks north and three blocks west from his house. Up until four years ago the high school kids would park on his street. It used to bother him, the crowds of kids leaving their cigarette butts stamped out on his sidewalk or in his lawn, the lawn the kids would trample as they cut through his yard. Now, though, he would be able to sit and watch, like he did with Amanda. For awhile now, she'd be in her driveway working on her free throws and layups and jumpers. She'd be out there late at night, the garage door open and the lights making her a shadow shooting baskets. She seemed so skinny, so slight, that he wondered if she could really play, if she could hold her own. Then, a couple of years ago, after Mr. Hawkins left his wife and Amanda for a faraway woman, Amanda shoveled the snow in the driveway and she played later and later at night, stopping only when her mom's headlights turned into the driveway as she came home from her four-to-midnight shift at the hospital.

It was five in the evening as Mr. O'Conner dragged his body through the neighborhood streets to get to the high school. The streetlights hadn't taken over completely, which meant that he could find the cracks and gaps in the sidewalk on the way there. When he was finally able to turn west, he needed to rest. He stopped for a few moments and he tried to remember the last time he just walked through the neighborhood. He couldn't pinpoint a memory. Three blocks to go, and even though he felt the excitement, he didn't realize how tired he'd feel. He started on his way again, determined to enjoy himself.

The parking lot at the high school was beginning to fill, and the kids moved and talked quickly with one another. They all wore green and black, the color of choice for the Lancers of Logan High. Making his way to the gym doors, he began to sweat, nervous and tired. The exercise should have felt good, but his legs burned and the joints throughout his body ached.

The gym was cast in a yellow fluorescent light, and it was warm. The pep band was assembling itself for the evening of two basketball games, first the girls and then the boys. The girls from both teams were on the floor warming up and he wished he could move like them, so free and quick and fluid. He took only a few steps into the gym and luckily found a seat near the gym door. The bleachers were hard and he couldn't lean back, but he was glad to be sitting. The bench for Logan was across the floor from him.

"Hi, Mr. O'Conner." A hand tapped his shoulder and it was Mrs. Hawkins, a woman with plump cheeks and friendly brown eyes. "It's good to see you."

"Hi," he said, taking off his cap and wiping down the sweat.

"Tonight's Senior Night," she said, "That's why I've got on the corsage."

He nodded his head. She was talking to him, but he was still trying to catch his breath. His undershirt felt damp.

Amanda sat on the end of the bench. Her knee was swollen and puffed up about the size of a grapefruit. She was clapping, cheering on her teammates, trying to get them excited and focused on the game. She was about five foot six inches, but he guessed that she didn't weigh more than 120 pounds. Her hips were still narrow, which made the knee seem even bigger when she stood. But there she stood with her black hair pulled back, her large eyes focused on the task at hand. Even hurt, she seemed like a leader. She wasn't just part of the team, he figured, she guided it.

He was breathing easier now, but his legs were tired. "Excuse me, Mr. O'Conner." She put her hand on his shoulder again. This time, though, she was standing and then she was stepping down on the bleacher next to him. "They need me on the court."

The teams ended their warm-ups and the announcer asked for everyone's attention at half court. Standing there was Mrs. Hawkins with two other women and two men. "Tonight," the announcer said, "is the final home game for three of our seniors." The half-filled gym began to cheer and the entire boys' team stood and clapped. "And we'd like to acknowledge their parents."

When the first two names were called, the girls jogged out to their parent, kissed them on the cheeks, and gave the mom a single rose. A photographer stood to the side and seemed like he knew how to filter the fluorescent light for the shots. Then the announcer said, "Senior Captain Amanda Hawkins and her mother Pamela Hawkins."

Amanda was wearing her uniform, and she walked slowly and from behind it seemed like her shoulders were shaking. Mrs. Hawkins walked toward Amanda and met her halfway. Mrs. Hawkins hugged and clutched her daughter, and Mr. O'Conner saw her whisper, "I'm so proud of you." It would have been a great shot, a picture the two Hawkins women would cherish. Amanda hung on and as they both walked back to the bench, he could see that Amanda said, "Thanks, Mom."

The moment didn't last long, only a few seconds or so, and even though there were a couple of hundred fellow witnesses, Mr. O'Conner never longed so much for someone to thank him, someone to tell him how proud they were of him.

During the game, the gym began to fill because of the boys' game that would follow. Amanda cheered and seemed happy to be there. Mrs. Hawkins continued to cheer loudly throughout the game, even though Logan was losing by fifteen in the fourth quarter. He was more sore than ever. His back began to slouch. His neck was tired and he closed his eyes more than a couple of times as he took deep breaths. He began to wonder how long it'd take him to get home, and he started to put on his jacket and cap. He struggled to get out of the bleachers, but soon he was shuffling his way through the parking lot. Some kids were still coming into the gym and the headlights were still turning in to park. It was colder than earlier, but the moon was full and he could see his breath in the cold air.

"Mr. O'Conner, Mr. O'Conner," Mrs. Hawkins said from behind him. "When Amanda is done in the locker room, we're headed home. Would you like a ride?"

He nodded his head. "Yes," he said.

"We're right over here," she said, taking his arm.

On the drive home, he wanted to talk. He wanted to tell them about his son. He wanted to tell them about how lonely he had been and about how he used to watch Amanda shoot baskets for hours. He wanted to teach them the lessons about lights he had heard from his father: wavelengths affecting the color, black-and-white photographs play with the intensity of light, physicists define light as bundles of undulating energy. He just wanted to talk.

Instead, he sat in the passenger seat, buckled up, and his chin resting on his chest. He caught himself almost falling asleep.

"Amanda, are you OK?" Mrs. Hawkins asked.

"I just want to get home."

"Are you going to be all right by yourself tonight?"

"Is Mr. O'Conner OK?"

He could tell that they were both looking at him, but he didn't say anything.

"We're here Mr. O'Conner." Mrs. Hawkins looked at her daughter. "Can you walk him across the street?"

Amanda opened his door. He turned his body in the seat and Amanda took his hand. She helped him up as he used his other hand on the other door to give himself leverage.

"You guys OK?"

"No problem, Mom. See you when you get back."

"I'm sorry dear."

"Go to work, Mom, don't worry."

Even though he knew her knee was hurt, he couldn't help but lean on her as the walked. They would have been a good shot as they passed under the street light: a large, hobbled old man leaning on a seventeen-year-old girl who had one good leg and probably weighed less than his belly. When they got to the door, he said, "It's dark. Find the right key please. Can you turn on the light too?"

She seemed so short, so small, so fragile, and even though her eyes were large and friendly like her mom's, he knew that Amanda was also strong. "I wish I could have seen you play tonight."

"Me, too." She turned on the light by the door. "Can I do anything else for you?"

He slowly made his way to the leather chair. "Water. Can you get me a glass of water?" He plopped down and breathed heavily. He tilted his head back.

"Here you go," she said.

He took the glass and a large swallow of water. She sat on the couch, her hands resting in her lap. He put the glass down on the table and turned on the table lamp. "It must have been hard for you tonight, watching your last game."

Amanda shrugged her shoulders. "You've got a lot of pictures in here. Are they all your family?"

"Mostly."

"That's Mrs. O'Conner and that's your son, right?"

He nodded his head and sighed. "I like black-and-white photos," he said, "because the intensity of the light is critical for a good shot."

"Oh."

"You see that picture over there by the light switch?"

"The big one in the gold frame?"

"That's my father, and he's the one who gave me the photography bug. He taught me about light."

Amanda nodded her head and stared at the picture. "It's been three years," she said. "Tomorrow it'll be three years since he left." She closed her eyes, her lips open, her head shaking. Mr. O'Conner took a sip of water and then cleared his throat.

"It's tough, isn't it?"

She kept shaking her head. "I miss him. I'm pissed at him. I hate him for what he did to me and Mom. But I miss him. I'm so screwed up."

He took another sip and then he took off the cap. "Can you do this old man another favor?" he asked. "Can you tell me a story about you and him? No one tells me any stories anymore."

She rubbed her knee and grinned. "On one condition," she said.

He nodded.

"You have to close your eyes. The story is better when you close your eyes."

He leaned his head back and closed his eyes. She took a deep breath and he could hear her get up off the couch. She turned off the overhead light, sat back down, and turned off the table lamp between them. He imagined the silhouette of the tables and chairs and television.

"I was about nine and we were on vacation on the Atlantic somewhere in Florida. Even though it was evening, it was hot. We were on the beach, just us and he said to me, 'Close your eyes.' I thought he was going to tickle me, so I didn't at first, I think I even ran in front of him. When he caught up with me, he said, 'Come on. I'm serious. Close your eyes.' And he held my hand. I felt so safe. He raised my arm and said, 'Open your arms wide and listen.' He had this deep, soft voice. 'Do you hear the waves? Listen to them crash. Do you hear the seagulls? Listen to your heartbeat. Do you hear it? Do you feel it? Now take a deep breath. Just listen. The waves, the seagulls, your heartbeat. It's all connected, my dear. Everyone has her own soundtrack and this is the start of yours.' And I stood there, listening to the sounds, feeling the breeze off the water, soaking in the salt air. And so sometimes, when I miss him, I'll drive out into the cornfields or off to a lake, where nobody is, and I'll stand, close my eyes. And I'll listen, wishing that I could hear his voice in my ear."

When he opened his eyes, Amanda sat on the couch, arms wide open, her head tilted back. Even in the dark he could tell that she was trying to smile.

Unit from Rachel Bear
Boise State Writing Project Teacher Consultant and
Member of the Leadership Team for the
National Writing Project's
Literacy in the Common Core Initiative

Unit Title: Writing the College Essay Personal Statement

Unit Description (Overview Narrative): This unit was designed and taught for a twelfth-grade Advanced Placement Literature and Composition class. It is part of a larger semester exploration of the function and importance of stories and storytelling. As teachers of inquiry do, I am always revising and rethinking my inquiry questions, which are the center of inquiry instruction since they provide a purpose for reading, writing, and discussion in an inquiry classroom. As I have taught and reflected on this course and my inquiry questions over the last few years, it has become clear that stories and storytelling are central to the texts we read and the writing we do in the first semester of the course. This unit is the second unit in a semester-long exploration of the question: *How do stories matter?* The unit is placed where it is because of the college application early action deadline, but this type of writing, "stories about the writer," falls nicely early in the course as a means for students, and me, to get to know each other better as we build community.

The semester is organized as follows:

Semester Essential Question: How Do Stories Matter?

Unit One: What Do the Stories We Remember and Tell Reveal About Us?

- Texts = *Frankenstein* and other texts alluded to, responding to, or inspired by the novel (including poems, films, visuals, and critical essays)
- Analytical focus = patterns in literature, allusions, texts in conversation
- Writing focus = argumentative literary analysis

Unit Two: What Is Our Story? How Can We Best Represent Ourselves?

- Texts = sample college essays and professional models of creative nonfiction
- Analytical focus = form and substance of the college application personal statement, elements of style, and authorial purpose
- Writing focus = narrative writing

Unit Three: What Is the Truth? How Important Is Knowing the True Story?

- Texts = *The Turn of the Screw* and critical essays
- Analytical focus = style analysis of craft and structure, with a focus on narrative perspective/point of view
- Writing focus = argumentative style analysis

(continues)

(continued)

Unit Four: Who Has the Right to Tell a Story? How Can We Listen to Silenced Voices?

- Texts = *Things Fall Apart* and *Heart of Darkness*
- Analytical focus = narrative perspective, setting, theme
- Writing focus = multimodal, collaborative composing using the Internet; research

Unit Five: How Do Stories Matter?

- Texts = student-selected
- Analytical focus = texts in conversation
- Writing focus = researched literary analysis compare and contrast based on student-generated focus question (work on the Senior Research Project continues into the second semester)

This unit is designed to guide students through the process of creating a unique, meaningful, and effective college essay personal statement. The unit focuses on guiding students to understanding what makes a good college essay, the ways in which they can use narration and the elements of storytelling to reveal something meaningful about themselves, and the importance of writing an essay that will stand out. The module involves analyzing model essays (from other students and professional models), working from an abundance of writing, and engaging in guided, thorough revision activities. Students will understand the *purpose* of narrative writing, will be able to *name* the *features* and *content* of narrative writing and will be able to *produce* the *substance* and *form* of effective narrative writing.

Although this particular unit is for the college essay, the sequence and strategies could easily be adapted for any "Stories of One's Thought" in which they are "trying to capture two stories: the story of what happened and the story of how [they are] making sense of it now" (for more, see Bruner quotation in Chapter 3 about landscape and action and landscape and consciousness as well as Ballenger's idea in Chapter 5 about stories that describe what happened and reflect on what that action means). I have used these strategies and this instructional sequence for teaching various other types of narrative writing. Also, the activities are tied specifically to grade 11–12 CCSS Standards, but the equivalent standard at any grade level could be met with little or no modification of the instructional activities.

UNIT ESSENTIAL QUESTIONS:

What is our story? How can we best represent ourselves?

Grade(s)/Level:	Grade 12
Discipline:	English Language Arts
Course:	Advanced Placement English Literature and Composition
Author(s):	Rachel Bear
Contact Information:	rachel.bear@boiseschools.org

SECTION 1: STANDARDS

A. College and Career Readiness Standards (CCR) for Grade 11–12

Number	CCSS Standards for Reading Literature Grade 11–12
2	Determine two or more themes or central ideas of a text and analyze their development over the course of that text, including how they interact and build on one another to produce a complex account; provide an objective summary of the text.
3	Analyze the impact of the author's choices regarding how to develop and relate elements of a story or drama (e.g., where a story is set, how the action is ordered, how the characters are introduced and developed).
4	Determine the meaning of words and phrases as they are used in a text, including figurative and connotative meanings; analyze the impact of specific word choices on meaning and tone, including words with multiple meanings or language that is particularly fresh, engaging, or beautiful. (Include Shakespeare as well as other authors.)
5	Analyze how an author's choices affected structuring specific parts of a text (e.g., the choice of where to begin or end a story, the choice to provide a comedic or tragic resolution) contribute to its overall structure and meaning as well as its aesthetic impact.
7	Integrate and evaluate content presented in diverse formats and media, including visually and quantitatively, as well as in words.
Number	CCSS Standards for Writing Grades 11–12:
3	Write narratives to develop real or imagined experiences or events using effective technique, well-chosen details, and well-structured event sequences (see CCSS standard 3 for a–e).
4	Produce clear and coherent writing in which the development, organization, and style are appropriate to task, purpose, and audience.
5	Develop and strengthen writing as needed by planning, revising, editing, rewriting, or trying a new approach, focusing on addressing what is most significant for a specific purpose and audience.
10	Write routinely over extended time frames (time for research, reflection, and revision) and shorter time frames (a single sitting or a day or two) for a range of tasks, purposes, and audiences.
Number	CCSS Standards for Speaking and Listening Grades 11–12:
1	Initiate and participate effectively in a range of collaborative discussions (one-on-one, in groups, and teacher-led) with diverse partners on grades 11–12 topics, texts and issues, building on others' ideas and expressing their own clearly and persuasively. (See CCSS speaking and listening standard 1 a–d at the 11–12 grade level.)
2	Integrate multiple sources of information presented in diverse formats and media (e.g., visually, quantitatively, orally) in order to make informed decisions and solve problems, evaluating the credibility and accuracy of each source, and noting any discrepancies among the data.
4	Present information, findings, and supporting evidence, conveying a clear and distinct perspective, such that listeners can follow the line of reasoning, alternative or opposing perspectives are addressed, and the organization, development, substance, and style are appropriate to purpose, audience, and a range of formal and informal tasks.

SECTION 2: ASSESSMENT

Summative Writing Assessment

Background: It is common practice for high school seniors to be asked to write the college essay "personal statement" as part of the college application and/or scholarship application process. Although a very important and authentic writing experience for them, most students are left to plan, draft, revise, and submit this type of writing without any teacher guidance. This unit is designed to guide students through this process, assisting them through analysis of sample essays, modeling, and guided revision activities, in creating a final product that reveals, through story, something significant about who they are.

<u>**Prompt**</u>:

<u>**Essential questions:**</u> What is our story? How can we best represent ourselves?

After reading sample narrative essays representing a variety of stylistic and organizational choices, write a narrative essay that relates a significant life experience, demonstrating understanding of what is appropriate and effective for the task, purpose, and audience. Use stylistic devices (e.g., imagery, tone, humor, suspense) to develop your work.

Formative Assessment

Background: Formative assessments for this unit are blended throughout the sequence of lessons and are designed for teachers to evaluate whether each student can display, when working independently, understanding of writing concepts explored throughout the sequence of instruction.

<u>**Prompts**</u>:

1. After reading sample rubrics and scoring systems, write two possible drafts (sketches) that relate a significant, unique life experience.

2. After reading sample student essays, write two sketches that relate a unique significant life experience.

3. After reading sample student "Essays That Worked," write three possible leads that relate a significant and intriguing moment in the story.

SECTION 3: THE INSTRUCTIONAL LADDER

Five Kinds of Knowledge/ Five Kinds of Composing	Instructional Strategies	Common Core State Standards	See Page
What are the students getting after in terms of the five kinds of knowledge? What are the types of composing they are doing?	*What strategies and what sequence will apprentice students to the summative writing task?*	*When and through which strategies are the Common Core State Standards being taught?*	*Where in this book can we see explanation/ connections?*
Knowledge of Context and Purpose: Students begin to articulate the purpose, context, and audience for the college essay personal statement. **Composing to Plan:** Students set a purpose for writing through discussion of "hot topics" related to the college essay process, including the college essay personal statement	**Day 1:** • **Introduce questions:** What is our story? How do we best represent ourselves? • **Visual analysis of political cartoons:** Discuss challenges of the college application process. • **"Stand and deliver" discussion:** Respond to controversial statements about the college essay process.	Cite strong textual evidence to support analysis of what cartoon implies about the college application process. (R1) Participate in small-group discussion of controversial statements related to college application process, propelling conversation by posing and responding to questions and supporting with examples from own life and experience. (SL1, SL4)	Chapter 1, page 7 (Knowledge of Purpose, Composing to Plan) Chapter 3, page 60 (EQ and Purpose)
Procedural Knowledge of Substance: Students begin generating ideas for interesting and compelling content for their essays. **Conceptual Knowledge of Substance and Form:** Through analysis of sample scoring systems, students begin to articulate and name the features and kinds of topics that make for an effective college essay. **Composing to Practice:** In low-stakes "sketch" writing, students begin experimenting with a potential topic for the essay.	**Day 2:** • **Brainstorm:** List of stories we could tell to communicate "top ten me-shaping events." • **Write sketch 1:** Write a very early draft focused on getting the story down (about fifteen minutes worth of writing). • **Discussion:** Look at sample college essay scoring systems from actual colleges.	Brainstorm and plan possible topics that are appropriate to the college essay, appropriate to the purpose of revealing important information about self, and appropriate to the college admissions counselor as an audience. (W5) Write an early draft of a possible essay in a short time frame, with a focus on a unique and engaging topic that would appeal to a potential reader. (W10) Integrate and evaluate source of information in the form of rubrics and checklists for scoring essays in order to address the question of what a college essay admissions counselor, the audience for this type of writing, is looking for in an effective essay. (RI7, W10)	Chapter 1, page 7 (Kinds of Knowledge and Composing to Practice) Chapter 5, page 71 (Freewriting) Chapter 5, page 72 ("Me-Shaping Events")

(continues)

(continued)

Five Kinds of Knowledge/ Five Kinds of Composing	Instructional Strategies	Common Core State Standards	See Page
Knowledge of Purpose: Students are introduced to the clearly stated conceptual and procedural goals for the writing task. **Declarative Knowledge of Substance and Form:** Through creating a scoring system, students label their own criteria for the content and substance of this type of writing. **Composing to Plan:** Students create a scoring system that articulates their purpose, context, substance, and form of an effective essay.	**Day 3:** • **Create scoring system:** In small groups, develop scoring system to be used for evaluating sample essays. System may be modeled after a specific sample scoring system, a combination of some elements, or a new approach entirely. • **Introduce and discuss goals for unit and writing task.** • **Conceptual goal:** Name the features and content of an effective college application essay. • **Procedural goal:** Write five-hundred-word narrative essay that develops a real experience or event using effective technique, well-chosen details, and well-structured event sequences.	Engage in collegial discussion and make decisions in order to negotiate scoring system that accounts for the opinions of all group members, all under the time constraint of one class period. (SL1b) Present claims for what makes an effective essay, in a focused and coherent manner, with relevant evidence from own experience, and scoring systems and sound valid reasoning. (SL4)	Chapter 1, page 7 (Knowledge of Purpose and Context) Chapter 3, Substance of Stories
Knowledge of Purpose: Students analyze the many elements of a college application and consider the purpose of the personal statement within that larger context. **Procedural Knowledge of Substance:** Students begin generating ideas for interesting and compelling content for their essays. **Composing to Practice:** In low-stakes "sketch" writing, students begin experimenting with another potential topic for the essay.	**Day 4:** • **Share writing task description** with students • **Analyze** common application prompts. • **Discuss** elements of the college application and role of the essay. • **Minilesson:** Introduce importance of working from abundance and writing badly. • **Write sketch 2:** Form and process are the same as sketch 1, choose a different topic for this sketch.	Discuss and articulate the features and content (conceptual goal), form (procedural goal), purpose, and audience for this type of writing. (W4) Develop and strengthen writing by trying a new approach to the writing task. (W5)	Chapter 1, page 7 (Purpose and Kinds of Knowledge)

(continues)

Five Kinds of Knowledge/ Five Kinds of Composing	Instructional Strategies	Common Core State Standards	See Page
Declarative Knowledge of Substance and Form: Through modeling and gradual release of responsibility, students are supported in naming the content, structure, and features of an effective college essay. **Procedural Knowledge of Substance:** Students begin generating ideas for interesting and compelling content for their essays. **Composing to Practice:** In low-stakes "sketch" writing, students begin experimenting with another potential topic for the essay.	**Day 5:** • **Teacher-modeled think-aloud:** Use document camera to model reading and annotation of a sample college essay with a focus on "narrative features." • **Teacher and student think-aloud:** On document camera, work through remainder of sample essay, asking students to share what they notice about the choices the student has made regarding each of the narrative features. • **Write sketches 3 and 4:** Form and process are the same as previous sketches, but topic should be different. (Note: Sketch 4 can be assigned for homework if class time runs short.)	Integrate information presented orally and in writing in order to build understanding of how to analyze authorial choices regarding word selection, organization, structure, and effect on overall meaning in preparation for performing analysis with less assistance. (SL2) Analyze, in writing and speaking, how authorial choices (made by students in sample essays) regarding structure and organization, choice and use of words, and development of related elements contribute to overall meaning as well as its aesthetic impact and overall effectiveness. (RL3, RL4, RL5) Develop and strengthen writing by trying a new approach to the writing task. (W5)	Chapter 3, Substance of Stories and Chapter 4, Shaping the Substance of Stories
Declarative Knowledge of Substance and Form: Through application of scoring system and exposure to sample essays (good and bad), students name the content, structure, and features of an effective college essay. **Procedural Knowledge of Substance:** Students continue generating ideas for interesting and compelling content for their essays. **Composing to Practice:** In low-stakes "sketch" writing, students begin experimenting with another potential topic for the essay.	**Days 6/7:** • **Score sample essays:** In small groups, use group-created scoring system to discuss and score sample essays. • **Full-class discussion:** Share and discuss scores from experts and compare to own scores. • **Anchor chart:** Butcher paper chart of slide on PowerPoint, designed to track and refine thinking about topic. In this case, what makes a good college essay? • **Encyclopedia of ordinary life:** Brainstorm one more sketch idea. • **Write sketch 5** (revisit idea of working from abundance rather than scarcity and the importance of taking risks).	Analyze, in writing and speaking, how authorial choices (made by students in sample essays) regarding structure and organization, choice and use of words, and choice regarding how to develop and relate elements of a story contribute to overall meaning as well as its aesthetic impact and overall effectiveness. (RL3, RL4, RL5) Participate effectively in collaborative discussion, propelling conversation by posing and responding to questions that probe reasoning and evidence, responding thoughtfully with consideration of claims and evidence provided by peers. (SL1c, SL1d) Participate effectively in collaborative discussion of what makes a good college essay, providing evidence from sample essays to support argument. (SL1)	Chapter 5, pages 73–74 (Encyclopedia)

(continues)

(continued)

Five Kinds of Knowledge/ Five Kinds of Composing	Instructional Strategies	Common Core State Standards	See Page
Declarative Knowledge of Substance and Form: Through close analysis of one "Essay That Worked" and exposure to an additional "Essay That Worked," students continue to name and refine the content, structure, and conventions for this writing task. **Knowledge of Purpose:** Students refine and modify their understanding of the context and purpose of the writing task. **Composing to Plan:** Students prepare to apply knowledge of purpose and context to composing of initial drafts.	**Day 8:** • **Analysis of effective essays:** In small groups, read and annotate the "Essay That Worked" from Connecticut College. As reading, highlight use of description and reflection • **Visual representation:** Create a metaphorical, visual representation of essay organization and use of narrative features. • **Jigsaw discussion:** Meet with one or two other groups who have different essays. Compare and discuss visuals as well as the question: What are the possibilities for organizing an effective essay? • **Anchor chart:** Revisit butcher paper chart of slide on PowerPoint, designed to track and refine thinking about topic. In this case, what makes a good college essay?	Analyze how authorial choices regarding structure and organization, choice and use of words, and development of related elements contribute to an "effective" essay according to Connecticut College. (RL3, RL4, RL5) Use the concept of analogy, through creation of a visual representation, to demonstrate understanding of possible authorial decisions regarding organization of an effective essay. (W2d) Participate effectively in collaborative discussion, propelling conversation by posing and responding to questions that probe reasoning and evidence, responding thoughtfully with consideration of claims and evidence provided by peers. (SL1c, SL1d)	Chapter 5, page 74 (Articulating Criteria) Chapter 4, Shaping the Substance of Stories
Declarative Knowledge of Substance and Form: Students develop vocabulary for naming the features and content of "narrative of thought" writing. **Procedural Knowledge of Substance and Form:** Students choose most interesting and compelling content and begin initial draft composing with consideration of how to shape that content into conventional, interesting, and shareable form. **Composing First Drafts:** Students try out three possible beginnings for the essay and the first possibility for a fully formed draft.	**Day 9:** • **Minilesson:** Introduce vocabulary for talking about description and reflection: – Ladder of abstraction (filter and slant) – Snapshots and thoughtshots (action and commentary) • **Choosing a topic:** Engage in guided process for revisiting sketches and getting feedback from peers regarding what subject will fit the purpose and audience of the writing task. Choose topic. • **Writing the lead:** Engage in guided process for writing three possible leads for essay. • **Homework:** Write draft 1. Start with chosen lead and write a full, more developed draft of the essay. This draft should move beyond just trying to "get it down" and reflect consideration of sample scoring, sample essays (that worked and didn't work), and class discussion.	Develop and strengthen writing by focusing on what is most significant for the purpose and audience of a college essay personal statement. (W5) Develop and strengthen writing by trying several approaches to writing the lead to the essay. (W5) Develop and strengthen writing by revising, trying a new approach and rewriting. (W5)	Chapter 3, Substance of Stories Chapter 4, page 50 (Filter and Slant) Chapter 4, page 59 (Time) Chapter 4, page 48 (State of Mind) Chapter 5, page 73 (Ladder of Abstraction) Chapter 5, page 74 (Peer Responses) Chapter 5, page 81 (Choosing the Moment That Matters)

(continues)

Five Kinds of Knowledge/ Five Kinds of Composing	Instructional Strategies	Common Core State Standards	See Page
Procedural Knowledge of Form: Students begin shaping content into more compelling form through generating an abundance of writing through targeted revision strategies. **Composing First Drafts:** Students try out multiple possibilities for revising the draft. **Composing Final Drafts:** Students begin polishing writing to share with first audience, a peer, for response and conferencing.	**Day 10/11:** • **Peer conference:** Reflect on type of change that came about from event and extent to which it is communicated in the draft. • **Revision strategies** (model each first with my own story). • Engage in a variety of guided strategies designed to help students generate more writing, focused on specific skills necessary for writing an effective narrative. • Strategies include: – Adding snapshots and thoughtshots (filter and slant) – Exploding a moment (considering time) – Creating tension – Writing the ending – Sentence variety – Titles – Personal area for focal improvement in editing • **Homework:** Write draft 2, using writing generated during class on day 10/11.	Develop and strengthen writing as needed by rewriting, revising, and trying a new approach, focusing on addressing what is most significant for the purpose and audience of the college essay personal statement. (W5) Use narrative techniques, pacing, description, and reflection to develop experiences and events. (W3b) Use precise words and phrases, telling details, and sensory language to convey a vivid picture of the experience. (W3d) Provide a conclusion that follows and reflects on what is experienced, observed, or resolved over the course of the narrative. (W3e)	Chapter 2, page 13 (Narrative Features) Chapter 2, page 17 (Types of Change) Chapter 2, page 22 (Time) Chapter 5, page 75 (Editing)
Declarative Knowledge of Substance and Form: Students name content and features of effective narrative writing in analysis of peer essays. **(Prepare for) Composing to Transfer:** In peer conference, students receive feedback and have an opportunity to explain and justify their process, as well as point to specific passages in their drafts or to specific moments in their process that they learned from. **Composing Final Drafts:** Students further polish essay to share with second audience, instructor, for comments and evaluation through instructor's scoring system.	**Day 12:** • **Peer response:** Complete peer response. Specific and guided analysis of peer writing, focused on skills we have been working on throughout the unit. Include one personal area of focus in peer response. • **Peer conference:** Meet with peer and discuss responds and work together to brainstorm ideas for the reflective cover letter to be included with the final draft of the essay. • **Homework:** Apply peer suggestions to revise and write "final" draft of essay to be submitted to me for feedback.	Analyze how authorial choices made by peers regarding structure and organization, choice and use of words, and development of related elements contribute to the overall meaning and effectiveness of a piece. (RL3, RL4, RL5)	Chapter 5, page 74 (Peer Response)

(continues)

(continued)

Five Kinds of Knowledge/ Five Kinds of Composing	Instructional Strategies	Common Core State Standards	See Page
Procedural Knowledge of Substance and Form: Students make "final" decisions for content and shape of essay. **Composing Final Drafts:** Students further polish essay to share with second audience, instructor, for comments and evaluation through instructor's scoring system. **Composing to Transfer:** In cover letter, students reflect on composing process in order to transfer to new writing situations, including other college essays they need to write.	**Final Essay:** What is our story? How can we best represent ourselves? After reading sample narrative essays representing a variety of stylistic and organizational choices, write a narrative essay that relates a significant life experience, demonstrating understanding of what is appropriate and effective for the task, purpose, and audience. Use stylistic devices (e.g., imagery, tone, humor, suspense) to develop your work. Include reflective cover page with final draft of essay. Reflection should include areas of strength and possibilities for improvement, explanation and justification of composing process, and thoughts about how the processes they used in this essay can be transferred to other college essays they still need to write.	Write a narrative essay with a focus on engaging and orienting the reader, using a variety of techniques to sequence events to create a coherent whole, and build toward a particular tone and outcome. (W3a–d) Produce clear and coherent writing in which the development and organization are appropriate to the task, purpose, and audience. (W4)	Composing to Transfer sections of Chapters 5, 6, 7, and 8, as well as Chapter 9 (Narrative as a Mode of Inquiry)

Citations

Ideas for sequencing from Wilhelm (2007); Smith and Wilhelm (2010); Wilhelm, Baker, and Dube-Hackett (2001).

Ideas for model, mentor, and monitoring from Wilhelm (2007); Wilhelm, Wilhelm, and Boas (2009).

Ideas for generating ideas and revision from Lane (1993); Ballenger (2010).

Reflection Narrative	
What Worked	Overall, I was quite pleased with how the unit went. I really think it is valuable for students to see sample essays from other students and experience what it is like to read a lot of essays in one sitting. It really brings home the fact that what may seem very personal and significant to the individual, easily gets lost through writing to a stranger. I was also quite pleased with the series of revision strategies I used before the final draft. These really help students see what it means to genuinely revise and to work from abundance when redrafting. I overheard one student the day after this activity saying, "I have never done writing like what we did in class last time. That was really great." Also, for the most part, the final essays were well written and enjoyable to read. They did end up trying new things and engaging with new and varied techniques for writing narratives.
What I Would Change	In the past, I have pretty much just randomly chosen the sample student essays for the first round of scoring, as well as the sample student "Essays That Worked." In the future, I would be much more deliberate about the sample essays I choose. Although the scoring and discussion has gone well, I would think about what specifically I want them to see about the form and content of those essays and the many possibilities for handling those concepts effectively. Also, as is often the case, I want to do a better job of explicitly reflecting on the essential questions throughout and after completion of the writing process.

References

Anderson, J. 2007. *Everyday Editing: Inviting Students to Develop Skill and Craft in Writer's Workshop*. Portland, ME: Stenhouse.

Ballenger, B. 2010. *The Curious Writer*. Boston: Longman.

———. 2011. *Crafting Truth: Short Studies in Creative Nonfiction*. Boston: Longman.

Bancroft, T. 2006. *Creating Characters with Personality: For Film, TV, Animation, Video Games, and Graphic Novels*. New York: Watson-Guptill.

Barrett, H. C. 2004. Digital Storytelling. Retrieved October 30, 2011, from www.storycenter. org/index1.html.

Batson, S. 2007. *Truth: Personas, Needs, and Flaws in the Art of Building Actors and Creating Characters*. New York: Rugged Land.

Bell, L. A. 2010. *Storytelling for Social Justice: Connecting Narrative and the Arts in Antiracist Teaching*. New York: Routledge.

Bell, M. S. 1997. *Narrative Design: A Writer's Guide to Structure*. New York: W. W. Norton.

Bereiter, C., and M. Scardamalia. 1987. *The Psychology of Written Composition*. Hillsdale, NJ: Lawrence Erlbaum.

Bolter, J. D. 2001. *Writing Space: Computers, Hypertext, and the Remediation of Print*, 2d ed. Mahwah, NJ: Lawrence Erlbaum.

Booth, W. C. 1983. *The Rhetoric of Fiction*, 2d ed. Chicago: University of Chicago Press.

Borkan, J. M., W. Miller, and S. Reis. 1992. "Medicine as Storytelling." *Family Practice* 9 (2): 127–29.

Brooks, L. 2011. *Story Engineering: Mastering the Six Core Competencies of Successful Writing*. Cincinnati, OH: Writer's Digest Books.

Bruner, J. S. 1986. *Actual Minds, Possible Worlds*. Cambridge, MA: Harvard University Press.

———. 1991. "The Narrative Construction of Reality." *Critical Inquiry* 18 (1): 1–21.

———. 2002. *Making Stories: Law, Literature, Life*. New York: Farrar, Straus, and Giroux.

Campbell, J. 2008. *The Hero with a Thousand Faces*, 3d ed. Novato, CA: New World Library.

Center for Digital Storytelling. 2011. Retrieved October 30, 2011, from www.storycenter.org/ index1.html.

Chambers, T., and K. Montgomery. 2002. "Plot: Framing Contingency and Choice in Bioethics." In *Stories Matter: The Role of Narrative in Medical Ethics*, edited by R. Charon and M. Montello, 79–87. New York: Routledge.

Charon, R. 2006. *Narrative Medicine: Honoring the Stories of Illness*. Oxford, UK: Oxford University Press.

Chatman, S. B. 1990. *Coming to Terms: The Rhetoric of Narrative in Fiction and Film*. Ithaca, NY: Cornell University Press.

Clark, R. P. 2007. "The Ladder of Abstraction." In *Telling True Stories: A Nonfiction Writers' Guide from the Nieman Foundation at Harvard University*, edited by M. Kramer, W. Call, and Harvard University Nieman Foundation for Journalism, xvii, 317. New York: Plume.

Danko, S., J. Meneely, and M. Portillo. 2006. "Humanizing Design Through Narrative Inquiry." *Journal of Interior* Design 31 (2): 10–28.

Delgado, R. 1989. "Storytelling for Oppositionists and Others: A Plea for Narrative." *Michigan Law Review* 87 (8): 2411–41.

Dorfman, L. R., and R. Cappelli. 2007. *Mentor Texts: Teaching Writing Through Children's Literature, K–6*. Portland, ME: Stenhouse.

Dweck, C. S. 2006. *Mindset: The New Psychology of Success*. New York: Random House.

Dyson, A. H., and C. Genishi. 1994. *The Need for Story: Cultural Diversity in Classroom and Community*. Urbana, IL: National Council of Teachers of English.

Egri, L. 1960. *The Art of Dramatic Writing: Its Basis in the Creative Interpretation of Human Motives*. New York: Simon and Schuster.

Ellis, S. 2009. *Now Write! Nonfiction: Memoir, Journalism, and Creative Nonfiction Exercises from Today's Best Writers and Teachers*. New York: Jeremy P. Tarcher/Penguin.

Erickson, T. 1995. "Notes on Design Practice: Stories and Prototypes as Catalysts." In *Scenario-Based Design: Envisioning Work and Technology in System Development*, edited by J. M. Carroll, 37–58. New York: Wiley.

Fleischer, C., and S. Andrew-Vaughan. 2009. *Writing Outside Your Comfort Zone: Helping Students Navigate Unfamiliar Genres*. Portsmouth, NH: Heinemann.

Fletcher, R. J. 1993. *What a Writer Needs*. Portsmouth, NH: Heinemann.

Floden, R. E., and C. M. Clark. 1988. "Preparing Teachers for Uncertainty." *Teachers College Record* 89: 505–24.

Ford, R., ed. 2007. *The New Granta Book of the American Short Story*. London: Granta.

Frank, C., and L. B. Bird. 1999. *Ethnographic Eyes: A Teacher's Guide to Classroom Observation*. Portsmouth, NH: Heinemann.

Franklin, J. 1986. *Writing for Story: Craft Secrets of Dramatic Nonfiction by a Two-Time Pulitzer Prize Winner*. New York: Atheneum.

Fulford, R. 2000. *The Triumph of Narrative: Storytelling in the Age of Mass Culture*. New York: Broadway Books.

Gallagher, K. 2011. *Write Like This: Teaching Real-World Writing Through Modeling and Mentor Texts*. Portland, ME: Stenhouse.

Ganz, M. 2009. "Why Stories Matter: The Art and Craft of Social Change." Retrieved December 9, 2011, from http://friendsofjustice.wordpress.com/2009/02/18/marshall-ganz-why-stories-matter/.

Gardner, J. 1985. *The Art of Fiction: Notes on Craft for Young Writers*. New York: Vintage.

Harper, L. 1997. "The Writer's Toolbox: Five Tools for Activie Revision Instruction." *Language Arts* 74 (3): 193–200.

Hart, J. 2011. *Storycraft: The Complete Guide to Writing Narrative Nonfiction*. Chicago: University of Chicago Press.

Herman, D., B. McHale, and J. Phelan, eds. 2010. *Teaching Narrative Theory*. New York: Modern Language Association.

Hillocks, G. 1995. *Teaching Writing as Reflective Practice*. New York: Teachers College Press.

Hood, A. 1998. *Creating Character Emotions*. Cincinnati, OH: Story Press.

Hugo, R. 1979. *The Triggering Town: Lectures and Essays on Poetry and Writing*. New York: Norton.

Johnston, B. A. 2007. *Naming the World: And Other Exercises for the Creative Writer*. New York: Random House.

Keyes, R. 1995. *The Courage to Write: How Writers Transcend Fear*. New York: Holt.

Koch, S. 2003. *The Modern Library Writer's Workshop: A Guide to the Craft of Fiction*. New York: Modern Library.

Kramer, M., W. Call, and Harvard University Nieman Foundation for Journalism, eds. 2007. *Telling True Stories: A Nonfiction Writers' Guide from the Nieman Foundation at Harvard University*. New York: Plume.

Krull, K. 1996. *Wilma Unlimited. How Wilma Rudolph Became the World's Fastest Woman*. New York: Harcourt.

Kübler-Ross, E. 1969. *On Death and Dying*. New York: Macmillan.

Lamb, N. 2001. *The Writers Guide to Crafting Stories for Children*. Cincinnati, OH: Writer's Digest Books.

Lampert, M. 1985. "How Do Teachers Manage to Teach? Perspectives on Problems in Practice." *Harvard Educational Review* 55 (2): 178–94.

Lane, B. 1993. *After The End: Teaching and Learning Creative Revision*. Portsmouth, NH: Heinemann.

LaPlante, A. 2007. *The Making of a Story: A Norton Guide to Creative Writing*. New York: Norton.

Lattimer, H. 2003. *Thinking Through Genre: Units of Study in Reading and Writing Workshops 4–12*. Portland, ME: Stenhouse.

Lauther, H. 1998. *Creating Characters: A Writer's Reference to the Personality Traits That Bring Fictional People to Life*. Jefferson, NC: McFarland.

Lave, J., and E. Wenger. 1991. *Situated Learning: Legitimate Peripheral Participation*. Cambridge, UK: Cambridge University Press.

Levins Morales, A. 1998. *Medicine Stories: History, Culture and the Politics of Integrity*. Cambridge, MA: South End Press.

Massaro, T. 1989. "Empathy, Legal Storytelling, and the Rule of Law: New Worlds, Old Wounds?" *Michigan Law Review* 87 (8): 2099–2127.

Maynes, M. J., J. Pierce, and B. Laslett. 2008. *Telling Stories: The Use of Personal Narratives in the Social Sciences and History*. Ithaca, NY: Cornell University Press.

McClanahan, R. 1999. *Word Painting: A Guide to Writing More Descriptively*. Cincinnati, OH: Writer's Digest Books.

McCloud, S. 1993. *Understanding Comics: The Invisible Art*. Northampton, MA: Tundra Pub.

———. 2006. *Making Comics: Storytelling Secrets of Comics, Manga, and Graphic Novels*. New York: Harper.

McKee, R. 1997. *Story: Substance, Structure, Style, and the Principles of Screenwriting*. New York: Regan.

Meadows, M. S. 2003. *Pause and Effect: The Art of Interactive Narrative*. Indianapolis, IN: New Riders.

Morgan, N. 2003. *Working the Room: How to Move People to Action Through Audience-Centered Speaking*. Boston: Harvard Business School Press.

Morris, D. 2002. "Narrative, Ethics, and Pain: Thinking with Stories." In *Stories Matter: The Role of Narrative in Medical Ethics*, edited by R. Charon and M. Montello, 196–218. New York: Routledge.

Murphy, F. 2002. *General Washington and the General's Dog*. New York: Random House.

Pringle, L. 2000. *Bats! Strange and Wonderful*. Honesdale, PA: Boyd Mills Press.

Ray, K. W. 2011. *In Pictures and in Words : Teaching the Qualities of Good Writing Through Illustration Study*. Portsmouth, NH: Heinemann.

Rosenfeld, J. E. 2008. *Make a Scene: Crafting a Powerful Story One Scene at a Time*. Cincinnati, OH: Writer's Digest Books.

Rosenthal, A. K. 2005. *Encyclopedia of an Ordinary Life: Volume One*. New York: Crown.

Routledge Encyclopedia of Narrative Theory. 2005. Fabula: La Recherche en Litterature. Retrieved February 10, 2012, from www.fabula.org/actualites/routledge-encyclopedia-of-narrative-theory_10833.php.

Rubie, P., and G. Provost. 1998. *How to Tell a Story: The Secrets of Writing Captivating Tales*. Cincinnati, OH: Writer's Digest Books.

Rymes, B. 2009. *Classroom Discourse Analysis: A Tool for Critical Reflection*. Cresskill, NJ: Hampton.

Sauer, B. A. 2003. *The Rhetoric of Risk: Technical Documentation in Hazardous Environments*. Mahwah, NJ: Lawrence Erlbaum.

Schaafsma, D., R. Vinz, and National Conference on Research in Language and Literacy. 2011. *On Narrative Inquiry: Approaches to Language and Literacy Research*. New York: Teachers College.

Smith, M. W. 1991. *Understanding Unreliable Narrators: Reading Between the Lines in the Literature Classroom*. Urbana, IL: National Council of Teachers of English.

Smith, M. W., and J. D. Wilhelm. 2002. *"Reading Don't Fix No Chevys": Literacy in the Lives of Young Men*. Portsmouth, NH: Heinemann.

———. 2006. *Going with the Flow: How to Engage Boys (and Girls) in Their Literacy Learning*. Portsmouth, NH: Heinemann.

———. 2007. *Getting It Right: Fresh Approaches to Teaching Grammar, Usage, and Correctness*. New York: Scholastic.

———. 2010. *Fresh Takes on Teaching the Literary Elements: How to Teach What Really Matters About Character, Setting, Point of View, and Theme*. New York: Scholastic.

Smith, M. W., J. D. Wilhelm, and J. E. Fredricksen. 2012. *Oh, Yeah?! Putting Argument to Work Both in School and Out*. Portsmouth, NH: Heinemann.

Spinelli, J. 2000. *Stargirl*. New York: Random House.

Spradley, J. P. 1979. *The Ethnographic Interview*. New York: Holt, Rinehart, and Winston.

Stone, T. L. 2008. *Elizabeth Leads the Way: Elizabeth Cady Stanton and the Right to Vote*. New York: Holt.

Swain, D. V. 1990. *Creating Characters: How to Build Story People*. Cincinnati, OH: Writer's Digest Books.

Thomas, D., and J. S. Brown. 2011a. *A New Culture of Learning: Cultivating the Imagination for a World of Constant Change*. Seattle: Amazon/Createspace.

———. 2011b. "Cultivating the Imagination: Building Learning Environments for Innovation." Retrieved February 17, 2011, from www.newcultureoflearning.com/TCR.pdf.

Thompson, T. 2008. *Adventures in Graphica: Using Comics and Graphic Novels to Teach Comprehension, 2–6*. Portland, ME: Stenhouse.

Tizon, T. A. 2007. "Every Profile Is an Epic Story." In *Telling True Stories: A Nonfiction Writers' Guide from the Nieman Foundation at Harvard University*, edited by M. Kramer, W. Call, and Harvard University Nieman Foundation for Journalism, 71–73. New York: Plume.

Truby, J. 2007. *The Anatomy of Story: 22 Steps to Becoming a Master Storyteller*. New York: Faber and Faber.

Vorhaus, J. 1994. *The Comic Toolbox: How to Be Funny Even If You're Not*. Los Angeles: Silman-James.

Wiggins, G. P., and J. McTighe. 2005. *Understanding by Design*, expanded 2d ed. Alexandria, VA: Association for Supervision and Curriculum Development.

Wilhelm, J. D. 2001. *Improving Comprehension with Think-Alouds: Modeling What Good Readers Do*. New York: Scholastic.

———. 2002. *Action Strategies for Deepening Comprehension: Using Drama Strategies to Assist Improved Reading Performance*. New York: Scholastic.

———. 2004. *Reading Is Seeing: Learning to Visualize Scenes, Characters, Ideas, and Text Worlds to Improve Comprehension and Reflective Reading*. New York: Scholastic.

———. 2007. *Engaging Readers and Writers with Inquiry*. New York: Scholastic.

———. 2008. *"You Gotta BE the Book": Teaching Engaged and Reflective Reading with Adolescents*, 2d ed. New York: Teachers College Press.

———, ed. The Ten series. New York: Scholastic.

Wilhelm, J. D., T. N. Baker, and J. Dube-Hackett. 2001. *Strategic Reading: Guiding Students to Lifelong Literacy, 6–12*. Portsmouth, NH: Boynton/Cook.

Wilhelm, J. D., and B. Edmiston. 1998. *Imagining to Learn: Inquiry, Ethics, and Integration Through Drama*. Portsmouth, NH: Heinemann.

Wilhelm, J. D., P. Friedemann, and J. Erickson. 1998. *Hyperlearning: Where Projects, Inquiry, and Technology Meet*. York, ME: Stenhouse.

Wilhelm, J., and B. Novak. 2011. *Teaching Literacy for Love and Wisdom: From Being the Book to Being the Change.* New York: Teachers College Press.

Wilhelm, J. D., M. W. Smith, and J. E. Fredricksen. 2012. *Get It Done! Writing Informational Texts to Make Things Happen.* Portsmouth, NH: Heinemann.

Wilhelm, J. D., P. J. Wilhelm, and E. Boas. 2009. *Inquiring Minds Learn to Read and Write: 50 Problem-Based Literacy and Learning Strategies.* Markham, ON: Scholastic Canada.

Index

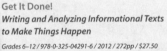